Freemasonry in Inverness

Also from Westphalia Press

westphaliapress.org

The Idea of the Digital University

Bulwarks Against Poverty in America

Treasures of London

Avate Garde Politician

L'Enfant and the Freemasons

Baronial Bedrooms

Making Trouble for Muslims

Philippine Masonic Directory ~ 1918

Paddle Your Own Canoe

Opportunity and Horatio Alger

Careers in the Face of Challenge

Bookplates of the Kings

The Boy Chums Cruising in Florida Waters

Freemasonry in Old Buffalo

Original Cables from the Pearl Harbor Attack

Social Satire and the Modern Novel

The Essence of Harvard

The Genius of Freemasonry

A Definitive Commentary on Bookplates

James Martineau and Rebuilding Theology

No Bird Lacks Feathers

Gems of Song for the Eastern Star

Crime 3.0

Anti-Masonry and the Murder of Morgan

Understanding Art

Spies I Knew

Lodge "Himalayan Brotherhood" No. 459 C.E.

Ancient Masonic Mysteries

Collecting Old Books

Masonic Secret Signs and Passwords

Death Valley in '49

Lariats and Lassos

Mr. Garfield of Ohio

The Wisdom of Thomas Starr King

The French Foreign Legion

War in Syria

Naturism Comes to the United States

New Sources on Women and Freemasonry

Designing, Adapting, Strategizing in Online Education

Gunboat and Gun-runner

Meeting Minutes of Naval Lodge No. 4 F.A.A.M ~ 1812 & 1813

Freemasonry in Inverness

Being an Account of the Ancient Lodges of
St. John's Old Kilwinning, No. 6 of Scotland
and
St. Andrew's Kilwinning, No. 31 of Scotland

by Alexander Ross

WESTPHALIA PRESS
An imprint of Policy Studies Organization

Freemasonry in Inverness
All Rights Reserved © 2014 by Policy Studies Organization

Westphalia Press
An imprint of Policy Studies Organization
1527 New Hampshire Ave., NW
Washington, D.C. 20036
info@ipsonet.org

ISBN-13: 978-1633910355
ISBN-10: 1633910350

Cover design by Taillefer Long at Illuminated Stories:
www.illuminatedstories.com

Daniel Gutierrez-Sandoval, Executive Director
PSO and Westphalia Press

Devin Proctor, Director of Media and Publications
PSO and Westphalia Press

Updated material and comments on this edition
can be found at the Westphalia Press website:
www.westphaliapress.org

FREEMASONRY IN INVERNESS:

BEING AN

ACCOUNT OF THE ANCIENT LODGES

OF

ST JOHN'S OLD KILWINNING,

No. 6 OF SCOTLAND,

AND

ST ANDREW'S KILWINNING,

No. 31 OF SCOTLAND

COMPILED FROM MINUTE BOOKS OF
THE LODGES BY

ALEXANDER ROSS, INVERNESS,
F.G.S., F.S.A. SCOT.,
R.W.M. OF ST JOHN'S LODGE.

―――――――

PRINTED, BY REQUEST OF THE BRETHREN, FOR PRIVATE CIRCULATION.

―――――――

INVERNESS:
PRINTED AT THE COURIER OFFICE.
1877

TO THE BRETHREN

OF

St John's Old Kilwinning Lodge of Freemasons, Inverness.

━━━◇━━━

DEAR BROTHERS,

I beg leave to lay before you the following account of Freemasonry in Inverness, and in doing so I trust you will kindly overlook its defects. It has no pretence to literary merit, consisting as it mainly does of extracts from the various minute-books, with a note here and there to connect them.

The task of selecting and preparing these for the press has occupied my leisure hours during the past winter months; but in copying out many of the minutes, I availed myself of the assistance of Mr Hugh C. Fraser, writer, and I have to thank him for the very careful manner he has done so, and also for many interesting notes made by him. I have also to thank Depute-Master Walter Carruthers, Mr W. R. Grant, solicitor; Mr Donald Reid, solicitor; and Mr George Wood for much valuable assistance and advice.

I am,

Yours fraternally,

ALEXANDER ROSS.

OFFICE-BEARERS FOR 1878,

ELECTED ST JOHN'S NIGHT 1877.

———◦◦┆◉┆◦◦———

R.W.M.—WALTER CARRUTHERS.

D.M.—H. C. MACANDREW.

Senior Warden—GEO. G. ALLAN.

Junior Warden—WM. BURNS.

Senior Deacon—A. T. F. FRASER.

Junior Deacon—WILLIAM JOLLY.

Treasurer—HUGH ROSE.

Secretary—DONALD REID.

Stewards—CHAS. SPINKS and JOHN MENZIES.

Inner Guard—J. G. BULMER.

Tyler—JOHN FOTHERINGHAM.

Past Masters—CHAS. INNES & ALEXANDER ROSS.

Chaplain—Dr MACDONALD, D.D.

Medical Officer to Society—J. WILSON, M.D.

LIST OF MEMBERS

OF

ST JOHN'S LODGE.

————∘⚬⁚✪⁚⚬∘————

The following is a list of the Members of St John's Lodge
at 27th December 1877:—

Date of Initiation.

12th Oct. 1825—Alex. Inglis Robertson of Aultnaskiah.

27th Dec. 1826—Joseph Mitchell, C.E., Inverness.

20th Nov. 1832—Duncan Mactavish, Heathmount, Inverness.

28th Dec. 1840—William Mackenzie, of the Union Lodge,
　　　　　　　Inverness.

　　　　　1852—John Fotheringham, Tyler (affiliated).

30th Nov. 1852—Alex. Simpson, Provost of Inverness.

　　　　,,　　　—James Simpson, Sheriff-Substitute, Fort-
　　　　　　　William.

　　　　,,　　　—Alexander Dallas, Town-Clerk.

30th Nov. 1854—Æneas Mackintosh of Daviot, Devon
　　　　　　　Cottage, Inverness.

27th Dec. 1854—William Ross Grant, solicitor, Inverness.

　　　　,,　　　—Colin Campbell, waiter, do.

26th Jan. 1855—Dr Robert Clark, Sierra Leone, now in
　　　　　　　Inverness.

20th June 1855—Rev. Dr Macdonald, First Minister of the
　　　　　　　Parish of Inverness.

　　　　,,　　　—Charles Spinks, Inverness (affiliated).

26th Nov. 1856—John Russell, Melbourne.

1st Dec. 1856—James Anderson, Procurator-Fiscal, In-
　　　　　　　verness-shire.

　　　　,,　　　—John Wilson, M.D., Inverness.

19th Nov. 1858—William Lawrie, architect, Inverness.

13th Jan. 1859—Henry Cockburn Macandrew, Sheriff-Clerk
    Inverness.

1st Feb. 1859—Donald Colin Cameron, tacksman of Tal-
    lisker, Isle of Skye.

19th Jan. 1860—Malcolm Maclennan, Procurator-Fiscal,
    Wick.

  ,, —John Colvin, solicitor, Inverness.

5th April 1860—Alfred Philip Biscoe.

1st Dec. 1862—Robert Carruthers, printer and publisher
    Inverness.

  ,, —Hugh Rose, solicitor, Inverness.

26th Nov. 1863—Alex. Maclennan, distiller, Ord (affiliated).

  ,, —Theo. James Bulkeley, Procurator-Fiscal,
    Lochmaddy.

  ,, —Charles Innes, solicitor, Inverness.

  ,, —Alex. Ross, architect, do. (affiliated).

30th Nov. 1863—Lewis Alex. Inkson, solicitor, do.

    —Walter Carruthers, publisher, do.

3rd Nov. 1864—James Menzies, Annesley, Newington,
    Edinburgh.

15th Dec. 1864—Andrew Dougall, manager, Highland Rail-
    way, Inverness.

23rd Dec. 1864—Frank Dawson Mitchell, C.E., Gampola,
    Ceylon.

27th Dec. 1864—James Rose, wine-merchant, do.

2nd April 1865—William Reid, architect, do. (affiliated).

29th Sept. 1865—Frederick David Rait, of No. 34 Buchanan
    Street, Glasgow.

19th Nov. 1865—Francis William Wisdom, Castle Street,
    Inverness (affiliated).

28th Nov. 1866—Captain William Douglas Bunbury, Willow
    Bank, Inverness.

  ,, —Charles Vernon Jenkins, captain, Bengal
    Artillery Corps.

  ,, —John C. Macewen, Inverness.

30th Nov. 1866—Carl Fleckstein, German and music master,
    Perth.

3rd Feb. 1869—John Menzies, Caledonian Hotel, do.
    (affiliated).

3rd Dec. 1869—William Donaldson, major, Inverness-shire
    H.L.I. Militia (affiliated).

3rd Dec. 1869—Donald Reid, solicitor, Inverness
  ,,   —William Tavish Mactavish, solicitor, Tain.
10th Dec. 1869—George Grant Allan, inspector of branches,
              Caledonian Bank, Inverness.
27th Dec. 1869—William Stroudley, superintendent of loco-
              motives, Brighton.
21st Oct. 1870—Adam Scott Reid, M.B. and C.M.
27th Nov. 1871—Angus Mackintosh of Holme.
4th Feb. 1873—Allan Macdonald, solicitor, Inverness.
  ,,   —William Macdonald, M.D., do.
6th Mar. 1874—William Burns, solicitor, do.
20th Oct. 1874—A. P. Mackenzie, Gairloch, Townsville,
              Queensland.
24th Oct. 1874—James Barron "Courier" Office, Inverness.
26th Dec. 1874—George G. Tait, solicitor, Tain.
7th Aug. 1875—Patrick Alex. Weir, A.M., M.B., C.M.
  ,,   —William Jolly, H.M. Inspector of Schools,
              Inverness.
  ,,   —Archibald T. F. Fraser, clothier, do.
2nd Sept. 1875—John George Bulmer, Highland Railway,
              Inverness.
4th Dec. 1875—Thomas Aitken, M.D., District Asylum,
              Inverness.
  ,,   —Donald Syme, H.M. Inspector of Schools,
              Bonar-Bridge.
  ,,   —Daniel James Mackay, solicitor, Inverness.
20th May 1876—John G. Davidson, C.E., Clachnaharry.
4th Nov. 1876—David S. Buchan, 27 Change Alley, London.
  ,,   —Alex. Cowan, wine-merchant, Inverness.
30th Nov. 1876—John Macleod, H.M. Inspector of Schools,
              Elgin.
  ,,   —James Ross, solicitor, Inverness.
16th Dec. 1876—William Mackay, solicitor, do.
23rd Dec. 1876—Evan George Mackenzie, solicitor, do.
5th May 1877—John Macandrew, Lahore (affiliated).
17th Nov. 1877—John Macfarquhar, M.A., Sheriff-Clerk-
              Depute, Inverness.
  ,,   —Robert H. Grant, solicitor, do.
  ,,   —Francis Foster, surveyor of taxes, do.

INTRODUCTION.

———∘∘⚬⚬∘∘———

Last year I undertook to look into the records of the Lodge, and after some difficulty I managed to collect a large portion of the minute books. These are now in the possession of the Lodge, and I trust that for the future they may be better cared for. The earliest records which I have been able to find, and which bring the Lodge prominently into notice, begin in 1678—the date of our present charter. That the Lodge of St John's is much older there can be no doubt, and there is a ready explanation of this comparatively modern date given in a petition sent to the Grand Lodge of Scotland in 1737. This document states that "previous to 1678 the Lodge kept their minutes from time to time in ane irregular manner, upon sheets and baffles of paper, most of which now we cannot collect so as to make any of them to purpose." At this time, however, a minute book was presented by the Honourable William MacIntosh, Broyr.-German to the Laird of MacIntosh, from which date all regular meetings and transactions are recorded. This minute book is unfortunately amissing, but of this I shall give a fuller account hereafter.

Having got back to the beginning of our own Lodge history, I was tempted to inquire into the history of masonry in a wider field, and having devoted a little time to the working out of the subject, I have thought it might not be uninteresting to the brethren if I threw a few rough notes together and read them for their amusement and instruction.

Naturally one looks back to the mother Lodge of Kilwinning, and so back to the 11th and 12th centuries, where I think the distinct records of Freemasonry, as we understand it, begin.

That Freemasonry, or some secret societies akin to it, have existed from the very earliest ages of the world, seems undoubted; but whether we can connect these by a regular succession with the Freemasonry of the middle ages or the present day, seems to me very doubtful; for, except as a secret society or in the principles of secrecy, the character of Freemasonry is much changed within comparatively recent times. A modern writer* says—"The universal prevalence of his secret principle, in both ancient and modern time is of itself a most significant fact, and could not have existed in all ages, and arrested the sympathie of the purest and best of men, unless it had respond d, in a degree at least, to some of the most

---

* See A old's "History and Philosophy of Freemasonry, and other Secret Societies."

urgent and vital needs of humanity.'' In Egypt we find them celebrating their mysterious rites in the Temple of Isis, in the heart of the Pyramids, round the sarcophagus of the murdered Osirus; in Greece, the mysteries of Orpheus and Elusinia; in North Europe, the Druidic and Odinic mysteries.'' Associated with these mysteries or secret societies we find the religion, wisdom, science, and knowledge of the period.

In their secluded lives they studied astronomy, philosophy, science, and the mysteries of nature, and established laws to order and govern their body and regulate the ceremonies of initiation, and I think the resemblance between the theme of the ceremony of the initiation of these bodies and those of Freemasonry are, to say the least, most remarkable.

I shall quote a description of the rites of the Cabiri of Samothrace.—

"After a previous probation of abstinence, chastity, and silence, the candidate for initiation was purified by water and blood. He then offered a sacrifice of a bull or a ram, and, as in Isianic rite, was made to drink of two fountains called Lethe (oblivion) and Mnemosyne (memory), to enable him to wash away his previous guilt, and to remember the new instructions. He was then conducted to a dark tower or cavern, and made to accomplish the mystic journey through gloom and terror, during which he met with the most frightful adventures. The most appalling sounds assailed his ears, the rushing of waters, the roar of thunder, and dreadful yells, while occasional gleams of light flashing through the darkness revealed to his view the most horrible phantoms. At length he found himself in a vast hall, in solemn silence and darkness. Presently a feeble light diffused a pale and spectral glare through the apartment, affording him a confused and dim view of the objects surrounding him. The walls were clothed with black drapery, and everything appeared the symbols of death, and decay and death—those emblems that point to the grave and speak eloquently and impressively of the supreme hour of man's worldly life, and of the exceeding vanity and emptiness of all sublunary enjoyments and pursuits. Terrific phantoms, grim and ghostly, passed and repassed before him. A bier rose up at his feet, on which was a coffin, and in the coffin a dead body! At this stage of the proceedings a funeral dirge was chanted by an invisible choir, and thus the sounds of terror and spectral visions were multiplied around him with rapid alternations until the proper effect was supposed to have been produced on his mind. Sometimes the neophyte was so overcome with fear, that he fell senseless on the ground. The pilgrimage of gloom and horror here ended—a flood of dazzling light now poured in upon the scene, which was changed as by enchantment.

"The dark drapery, with its startling devices and funeral emblems, had disappeared, and garlands of flowers and foliage adorned the walls and covered the altars; the dead body on the bier returned to life; the funeral psalm gave place to a song of hope and victory; and the ceremonies which had commenced in gloom and darkness, ended in light, and joy, and confidence.

"After these ceremonies had been performed, the candidate was led to the presiding priest, and instructed in the mystic science of the institution—theology, morals, philosophy, and politics being embraced in these instructions.

"To appreciate the utility of these mysteries, and their value as instruments or means of instruction, it is necessary to consider that the ancients in all their instructions, whether moral or religious, employed less of words and more of the language of signs, of solemn shows and symbols, and dramatic representation, than do the moderns. All great truths were inculcated, enforced, and elucidated through the medium of the Drama."

I have quoted these at some length, as I think that the same theme and character can be, to a certain extent, traced through all stages of the history of our secret societies, and if we cannot actually mark the connection of these bodies with our modern societies step by step, yet it is not difficult to believe that they were perpetuated in varying forms, as circumstances might render advisable and necessary. I have, perhaps, said enough to show to the initiated that a curious resemblance is traceable throughout the whole line, and to indicate that an interesting field of research is open to the student of these mysteries. That students have not been wanting to work in this field is abundantly proved by the many publications on the subject, but I confess myself unable to follow them up. They are more interesting than convincing; and the more exact records of Freemasonry, such as are contained in our own minute books, possess greater attraction for me. Among early notices of guilds or societies of craftsmen occur those in the third and fourth centuries of the Collegia Fabrorum and Collegia Artificium of Rome, framed after those of Greece, with their artificers and priests, their secret rites and laws. These closed societies were called upon to build cities and temples, and some of their associates accompanied each legion of Roman soldiers. The collegia consisted of architects, sculptors, and painters, and they were free from taxation.

I shall now briefly notice one or two allusions to Freemasonry in the middle ages, and note how they bear on our modern ideas of the subject. The earliest references, implying the existence of a regular Lodge, according to our ideas of the craft, occur about the eleventh and twelfth centuries. They lead us to infer that the erection of our great cathedrals, the Hôtels de Ville, and public buildings of the middle ages, was their work, or at least that of guilds or lodges of men who held charters and possessed privileges. One writer, Gerbert, a Benedictine monk (afterwards Pope Sylvester), who possessed much mathematical learning, which he obtained at Cordova and Granada, and seems to have induced a great change in the progress of learning during the tenth century. From the fifth century till his time (A.D. 999) the practice of architecture was a mere imitation of ancient Roman work, and there is a blank as to Freemasonry. The Crusaders made Western Europe acquainted with the science and knowledge acquired in the East, and it is recorded that in 1099 a certain Bishop of Utrecht was killed by the father of a young Freemason, from whom the prelate had exacted the mystery (Arcanum magisterium) of laying the foundation-stone of a church. The Freemasons of the middle ages seem to have been favoured by the Church, for letters of indulgence were granted to Ernest von Steinbach, the architect of Strasburg Cathedral, in 1278, by Pope Nicolas III. This Ernest von Steinbach had privileges conceded to him by Rudolph of Hapsburg, and the Lodge was regularly constituted, with power round a certain extent of territory to maintain order and obedience amongst the brethren under its jurisdiction, and these powers were renewed by the Popes until the fourteenth century. This is one of the earliest authentic records I know of the distinct formation of a Mason Lodge according to our modern ideas.

We have accounts of such fraternities being

formed in England—at Winchester and Canterbury
in 1202 and 1429—and the Freemasons of the
middle ages are credited with travelling up and down
Europe, under authority of the Pope, building the
various ecclesiastical buildings. This seems, however, open to some doubt; in fact, the national
characteristics of each country rather negative it.
The Gothic of Scotland is different in spirit and de-
velopment from that of England, and both are different from that of France and Germany, clearly proving
them the work of different peoples, though actuated
by the same motive and object; and though, perhaps,
one may doubt the general moving of bodies of Free
masons, yet there is abundant evidence of individuals
being induced to settle from time to time as required
at the various works. Another point in favour of
travelling bodies may be brought forward from the
fact that the mason's work, unlike most other artificers, must be done on the spot, and hence the
builders would have to travel to it. Yet, I am disposed to think the movements · must have been to
a large extent confined to countries and nationalities,
instead of continents.

The earliest allusion to travelling Freemasons is
made by one Aubrey, in the seventeenth century.
Writing in 1686, he says they were authorised by
the Pope. Search has been made in the Vatican for
the bull or patent on which the statement was said
to have been founded, but unsuccessfully; and it is

supposed to have referred to the letters of indulgence before referred to, and granted to Ernest von Steinbach.

It would appear to me rather that each cathedral had a complete staff of its own, and took on extra hands as required. This view is well authenticated, and the workmen at these buildings seem to have had special protection, as at Stratford-on-Avon, where the protection extended to the completion of the building, A.D. 1353.

The Freemasons of the middle ages are said to have enjoyed the protection and friendship of the Church; but latterly they showed themselves hostile to the monks, and this feeling would be aggravated when the Church withdrew her countenance from all secret societies. This has been assigned as an explanation of many of the grotesque figures and obscene carvings which disfigure our cathedrals. The monks and clergy having become the object of ridicule and dislike to the masons, these sculptures are so many caricatures or lampoons on their excesses. And this seems a reasonable explanation of a matter which has long puzzled antiquaries and architects. At Strasburg the masons have represented the priest as an ass saying mass, attended by other animals as acolytes, and as the work must have been done under the eyes of the monks themselves, it is difficult to account for the freak in any other way. Numerous instances might be quoted of these grotesque figures, both in England and Scotland, notably at Canterbury,

Elgin, Melrose, and even at St Clement's, the old
church at Rodil, in the Island of Harris.

From the number of acts passed to regulate wages
and to prevent combinations, it is clear that these
guilds had come to exercise a considerable influ-
ence; for in the time of Edward III. and Henry VI.,
masters, wardens, and people of guilds and fraternities are warned against making "amongst themselves unlawful and unreasonable ordinances for
their singular profit and the common damage of the
people." York claims to have received a charter of
incorporation from King Athelstane in 926, but, as
before said, there does not seem to have been any
authentic constitution of a lodge before that of Strasburg in 1278. York, however, possesses a continuous
list of master masons from 1347: they were duly
sworn to the office, they had a fixed salary, and
were pensioned when old and unfit for work. The
master was allowed a gown lined with fur, and tunics
were provided for the men, and gloves at 1½d. each.
The carpenters had aprons and clogs, and occasional
potations and remuneration for extra work.

Gwilt says—"The trades seem to have kept themselves distinct from a very early period. Thus, while
the monasteries had masons and carpenters, and a
plumber and his boy at hand, yet the glazier, bell-
founder, painter and decorator, smiths, and some
others were resident in the town or some adjoining
city."

Regarding the Lodges of Freemasons the probability is that these main centres formed the Mother Lodges from whence the smaller fraternities emanated whenever their skill was required, and they would naturally refer back to a hold of their Mother Lodge. These remarks are by no means meant to detract from the antiquity of Freemasonry, but are meant to show when and where occasional authentic glimpses may be found of the system. I may here make a remark on the origin of the name Freemason. In the fabric rolls of Exeter the word cementarius is used to signify mason down till 1360, and afterwards Freemason, which is said to designate a workman in freestone. My own impression is that the name is of French origin, and is meant to read Frère Maçon, signifying Brother Mason. Some of the words used in modern Lodges are evidently carried on from the practical usages of old Operative Masons. Thus, when they were to set about a work, they erected Lodges to work in and hold meetings, they thatched them and latterly tiled them, and they were then spoken of as "properly tiled," a word which we now employ to designate them as closed and secure, so as to prevent intrusion.

Before glancing at the early notices of Freemasonry in Scotland, I may remark, how natural it was that a body of men working under a master for many years should develop a system of fraternity or brother-hood, and how jealous the more proficient members would become of admitting younger members into their body. They insisted upon the youth serving a due apprenticeship, and at a time when education had made little progress, it is easy to understand how a system of signs came to be employed as a test by which to ascertain the position and progress of the various members. It was the practice that each mason should take up a distinctive sign or symbol by which he should be known, and by putting it on the stone, as he finished his task, the work of the different men could easily be identified. These marks seem to have been prevalent in all time, and they are found on the Pyramids of Egypt, the ancient buildings of India and Assyria, and so down through mediæval times to the present day; and in Freemasonry, as in actual work at the present day, they are also found. In one of the early records of St John's Lodge each one of our predecessors, as a member of the Lodge, put his mark after his name.

With regard to Freemasonry in Scotland, the earliest Lodge we have any record of is that of Kilwinning, in Ayrshire—Old Mother Kilwinning, as it is usually called—and the following statement is given in the Old Statistical Account of the parish, which, though not perhaps authentic in detail, yet it gives a plausible and not unlikely account of the matter :—

"Owing to the perishable nature of the buildings, principally of wood, up to the 10th and 11th centuries, the destructive and ruinous condition of many of the churches became a serious question, and the Pope created several corporations of Roman and Italian artisans, with high and exclusive privileges, especially with the power of settling the rates of prices of their labours, by their own authority, and without being controlled by the municipal laws of the country where they worked, and, in consequence of the exclusive privileges conferred on them, they assumed to themselves the name of Freemasons." "These corporations, whatever the origin of the name, possessed the power of taking apprentices and admitting into their body such masons as they approved of in the countries where they were engaged. And it is said a party established themselves at Kilwinning, and King James I. patronised the Mother Lodge at Kilwinning, and presided as Grand Master, till he settled an annual salary to be paid by every master mason, to a Grand Master chosen by the brethren and approved of by the Crown. It was required that the Grand Master should be nobly born, or a clergyman of high rank and character. He had deputes in different counties and towns in Scotland, and every new brother paid him a fee at entrance, and he was empowered to regulate and determine such matters in dispute between the founders and builders of churches and monasteries as it would have been improper to bring before a court of law."

King James II. conferred the office of Grand

Master on William Sinclair, Earl of Orkney and Baron of Roslyn, and afterwards made the office hereditary.

The Old Kilwinning Lodge continued to be the mother Lodge till 1736, when, at an assembly in that year, Lord Roslyn resigned the office as hereditary Master, at a meeting held at Edinburgh, when the Grand Lodge of Scotland was formed. At this meeting our Lodge of St John was represented, along with thirty-two others. Kilwinning Mother Lodge resisted this formation, and held independent meetings till 1807, when an arrangement was come to, and she relinquished her ancient claims and joined the general association.

The Kilwinning Lodge may be older than the fifteenth century, but their records do not go further back.

When the Cathedral system collapsed, Freemasonry seems to have fallen into disrepute throughout the greater part of Europe. The Church, hitherto its great supporter, began to discourage secret societies; the Lodges seem to have merged into guilds and incorporated trades, and in the beginning of the eighteenth century we find them existing in some way as part of these trades, though distinct as to secrets and rites. To so low an ebb had they reached that in 1737 there were only 34 Lodges remaining in Scotland, one of these being our own St John's. In 1727 a sudden movement was made, which rapidly spread over Europe, and Scotland was at this time looked upon as the cradle and nursery of Freemasonry, whence it rapidly spread over all the world.

The Old Lodge of York came forward and asserted its prior claim to that of Kilwinning, and a keen rivalry took place, but from the hazy condition of the evidence, it is difficult to say which had the best of it. The English Lodges hold off York, while all the Scotch acknowledge Kilwinning. The character of Freemasonry, as at this time established, was in many respects different from the older and more practical form. It became what might be called speculative Masonry, and men, other than craftsmen, were admitted to the secrets, and it is to be feared that, particularly on the Continent, Masonic meetings are used for political ends rather than for the cultivation of brotherly love and support. In this country, and in the present day, though preserving the secrets and rites of the fraternity, the cultivation of science has been lost sight of, and possibly the advance in education otherwise has rendered what was the seat and cradle of science unnecessary. Feelings of fellowship, brotherly love, the desire to help one another during life, and more than all, the wish to benefit the widows and children of members, have much to do with the maintenance of Masonry; and of this our own Lodge is a conspicuous example.

The extracts from our old minute books, and the light they cast upon social life in Inverness during the past two centuries, will, I trust, afford you some information as well as amusement. The quaintness of some of the entries must interest all, but especially those whose ancestors appear on the records and take part in the proceedings.

FREEMASONRY IN INVERNESS.

——∘∘ː◉ː∘∘——

The first account of Freemasonry in Inverness _{Prior to 1737} seems to be contained in a petition of the Old St John's Kilwinning—the Lodge of which we are members. This petition was framed in the year 1737, at the period when Freemasonry in its present shape was organised. About this time a movement to resuscitate Freemasonry was made throughout England and the Continent, and at this time also was formed the Grand Lodge of Scotland. On the occasion of its first meeting, held in Edinburgh on 30th November 1736, to elect a Grand Master, some 34 Scottish Lodges were represented. Old St John's Kilwinning of Inverness was represented by James Deans, master; Dr Thomas Horton and John Crawford, wardens. These were proxies, and the letter of James Deans undertaking the duty was as follows:—

"Dear Brother,—This day I was favoured with yours and honoured with your proxy, in execution of which I shall be carefull to act agreeable to your injunctions, and as becomes the dignity of your honble. Lodge. It gives me a great deal of pleasure to observe your good inclinations and zeal for the interest of Masonry, in making choice of my Lord Crawford, an excellent bro: and every way capable of that honble. office you have been pleased to name him for. But there are some inconveniences attending his election that you, because of your distance from Edinbr., probably have not had access to know, and therefor it is a duty incumbent on me to make you acquainted with them. First, My Lord went for London this morning, or is to set out to-morrow, and won't be in Scotland for a considerable time. 2d, It was proposed to his Ldship to stand candidate for the Grand Chair, but he declin'd it because he was obliged to attend Lord Illay to England, and was sensible nothing could be a greater loss to the first Grand Lodge than the absence of the G. Master. It is also the opinion of the brethren that to be perfectly unanimous in the choice of a G. M. will be altogether agreeable to that concord and harmony which wee cherish amongst us, and is the happy cement of our brotherly affections. I must also auquaint you that many of the Lodges have named my Lord Home (a bro. also verry well qualified) to be G. M., particularly Mary's Chapel, Glasgow; Hamilton, Falkirk, Dumfermling, and a great many more, so that it is without doubt my Lord Home will be elected. Therefor your proxy will be the only one for Ld. Crawford. I accquaint you with this only to exoner myself that you may know the opinions and designs of the othere Lodges, because probably you will think it convenient to join unanimously with the rest, and I believe, if I might humbly offer an advice, it will be best. I thought it was not proper to deliver your letter to the Four Master 'till I had accquainted you with what I have writ. But upon your answers (by the post) I shall exactly obey all your commands, either by a new proxy or by this I have received, as you shall be pleased to direct me.—I am, with sincere affect. to your honble. Lodge, R.W., your most humble servant and loveing bro.,   " JAMES DEANS.

" P.S.—Upon your recomendation, I shall be anxious to do Mr M'Queen what service lyes in my power. Receive a Book of Constitutions, which I borrd. from a bro., promising to suply him with one I have comissioned from London.

"Edinb., Nov. 16, 1736.

" D.B.—As the elections comes on Tuesday, the 30th instant, and that by course of the post cannot have your answer, and in consequence your proxy will be lost, wee entreat of you to renew it in favours of Lord Home, present Mr. of the Lodge of Kilnwinning, at the Scots Arms in Ed., and contrive to send it up so as it may be here on Monday, ye 29th, either by an express to the first post town or by some trusty private hand, for wee are aprehensive of some competition which we want to frustrate by all means possible. Take your own prudent measures to execute this, and you will oblige your affect. brothers, &c.,

" JAMES DEANS.

ALEXR. TAIT, S.W. of

"Nov. 18th."   Kilwinning, Scots Arms, Edinr.

(Addressed on outside)

" Mr Lauchlen Makintosh,

Mercht. in Inverness."

At the meeting of the Grand Lodge referred to, the resignation of Hereditary Grand Master was given in by William St Clair of Roslin, and he was immediately thereafter again chosen Grand Master. On St Andrew's day in the following year the Earl of Cromarty was elected to the office, and from this Grand Lodge it was enacted that all Lodges should for the future hold their charter.

In 1747, Inverness was erected into a Province, William Brodie of Brodie being Provincial Grand Master, the Lodges then in existence in the Province being—

> No. 6. Old Kilwinning, Inverness, whose charter dates from 1678, and which now ranks No. 6 of Scotland—clothing, dark blue, silver edge.
>
> 31. St Andrew's, Inverness, 1735, ceased 1837.
> 43. Fort-William, 1743, No. 43, orange and blue.
> 55. Brodie, Dyke, 1753, green.
> 57. Cumberland, Kilwinning, 1747, which was in existence in the year 1800.
>
> Other Lodges were created in the Province, viz.:—
> No. 115. Fort-George, Ardersier Point, 1763, ceased 1837.
> 259. Operative Clachnacuddin, 1796, ceased 1837.
> 350. Union, Inverness, —, ceased 1837, and the jewels and clothing came into possession of
> 339. St Mary's Caledonian Operative, Inverness, 1843, colour, green.

The latter is the only remaining Inverness Lodge, in addition to the St John's Old Kilwinning.

From the preceding list, it will be seen that Inverness has long been an active seat of Freemasonry, and I shall now proceed to glance through 1678 the minute books of the two Lodges, which form the St John's Kilwinning, viz., the Old St John's and St Andrew Lodges.

As before mentioned, Old St John's is not only the oldest Lodge in Inverness, but, in point of fact, it is the oldest Kilwinning Lodge now existing, our charter dating as from 1678, and none of the other Lodges dating before 1724.*

For more than a century the St John's and St Andrew's Lodges held their meetings in adjoining Lodges, and annually exchanged their deputations. As early as 1766, overtures were made for uniting their strength and building a Joint Lodge. This was accomplished in 1775; the foundation-stone of the new Lodge laid in 1776; and the building now known as the Caledonian Hotel was built and opened as an inn, under the name of the Mason Lodge, with the privilege we now possess of using certain rooms as our own Mason Lodge.

After the opening of the hotel the two Lodges kept a joint purse, and finally, in 1837, they conjoined their entire funds. In 1841 the scheme of the present St John's Friendly Society was projected and carried Friendly Society. out by Mr Joseph Mitchell and others, Mr Mitchell, however, taking a leading part as convener. The following is a list of members alive in 1853:—

Thomas Ross, general merchant, died in 1863.
Archibald Tait, perfumer, died in 1873.
John Thomson, banker, died in 1864.
George Mackay, merchant, died 19th May 1869.
John Mackay, banker, died 31st August 1861.

* See Laurie's History of Freemasonry.

Joseph Mitchell, C.E.

Robert Naughten, jeweller, died 18th April 1857.

Alexander Mactavish, town-clerk, died 1856.

James Grant Manford, writer, Forres, died 27th
November 1860.

Andrew Smith, merchant, died 1874.

Kenneth Douglas, bookseller, died 1860.

David Prophet, solicitor, died (in Australia) 1876.

James Macpherson, solicitor (who died 29th December 1867), was subsequently admitted in time to be recorded in the first list of the constituent members of the Society. The list of original members is given at page 221 of St Andrew's Lodge list. The Rules were revised in 1853, and again in 1877.

It may give a better idea of the progress and history of the Lodges if we take each separately, and select from their minutes the more prominent and interesting points as we proceed. And first, as to the minute books themselves. We learn from the petition before alluded to, that prior to the year 1678 the minutes of the St John's Lodge were kept in an irregular manner on loose pieces of paper, but from that year were engrossed in a minute book presented to the Lodge by William Mackntosh, brother to the Laird of Mackintosh. The loose memoranda have naturally disappeared in the course of two centuries, but it is matter of regret that the earliest minute book of the Lodge is also now missing. The oldest minute book in our possession commences in the year 1737, from which date our records are complete. It bears on its title-page—

"The Register of the Old Inverness Kilwinning Lodge of Freemasons, George Cuthbert of Castlehill,

Esq., Master, by whom gifted, this twentieth day of   1737
December, 1737 years."

In the year 1737, the Lodge being desirous of
obtaining a charter from the Grand Lodge, addressed
to it a memorial, a copy of which has been preserved,
and here follows, setting forth the succession of
office-bearers from the year 1678.

> "To the Most Worshipfull, The Grand Master
> and Bretheren of the Grand Lodge of Scot-
> land. The Memorial of the Old Kilwinning
> Lodge of Inverness.

"That preceding the year 1678, it seems by tra-   1678
dition of our oldest members now living, that the
Lodge keept their minuts from time to time in ane
irregular manner upon sheets or baffles of paper, most
of which we now cannot collect, so as to make anything of them to purpose—they haveing either been
cancelled or lost by accident.

"But upon the 27th December, 1678 years, Ther
was a book given in by The Honble. William M'Intosh (Broyr. german to the then Laird of M'Intosh),
who was then chosen Master of the Lodge, from
which date all the regular meetings & transactions of
the Lodge are recorded till this date.

"Inverness, 27th December 1678, William Mack-
Intosh was chosen Master, Alexr. Nicolson, Senr.,
Andw. Ross, Junr. Wardens, & Dd. Ross, boxmr.
The same persons continued in these offices till 15th
November 1681, when William Hendrie was chosen
boxmaster or Thesaurer, & the above members con-
tinued till 1st December 1684 when John M'Bean

¹⁶⁸⁴ was chosen Junr. Warden & Andw. Ross, Thesaurer, ye rest continued till

" 27th December 1692, when James Barbour was chosen Master, John Reid, Senr., and John Heburn, Junr. Wardens, and Andw. Ross, Thesaurer, and continued till

" 27th December 1699, when John Heburn was chosen Master, John Reid, Senr., and Robert Nicolson, Junr. Wardens, and Andw. Ross, Thesaurer, and continued till

" 27th December 1701, when James Dick was chosen Master, Andw. Ross, Senr., and William Cumming, Junr. Wardens, Alexr. Tulloch, Thesaurer, and continued till

" 28th December 1702, when the said James Dick was continued Master, Robert Nicolson and Alexr. Tulloch, Wardens, and John Thomson, Thesaurer, and continued till

" 6th August 1716, when Andrew Scott was chosen Master, James Dick, Senr., and John Dick, Junr. Wardens, and the said John, Thesaurer, and continued till

" 27th December 1718, when the said Andw. Scott was continued Master, Robt. Ross, Senr., and Thos. Tulloch, Junr. Wardens, and ye said Thos. Tulloch, Thesaurer, and continued till

" 28th December, 1719, when Donald M'Lise was chosen Master, Donald and Thomas Tulloch, Wardens, the Boxmaster continued, and ye rest, till

" 27th December 1722, when John Nicolson was chosen Master, Donald M'Lise, Senr., and John M'Bean, Junr. Wardens, and Alexr. Fraser, Boxmaster, and continued till

"28th December 1724, when John M'Bean was ¹⁷²⁴ chosen Master, Donald M'Lise, Senr., and John Jackson, Junior Wardens, and ye said John Jackson, Thesaurer, and continued till

"27th December 1733, when Bailly William M'Intosh was chosen Master, John Dunbar, Senr., and Alex. Fraser, Junr. Wardens, and the said Alexr., Boxmaster, and continued till

"27th December 1735, when John M'Bean was chosen Master, John Dunbar, Senr., and Alexr. Fraser, Junr. Wardens, and the said Boxmaster continued, &c., continued till

"27th December 1736, when George Cuthbert of Castlehill was chosen Master, John Dunbar, Senr., and Dond. M'Lise, Junior Wardens, and Alexr. Fraser, Thesaurer."

On the back of the copy of the petition which we have is the following indorsation :—

"In a full meeting of this Lodge, Inverness, 26th September 1737. Wee, the Master and Wardens hereto subscriveing, doe attest the above to be a genuine duplicate of the minutes of this Lodge, as the same stands recorded in the said minute book, deposited in the box by the Honourable William M'Intosh, Esquire, as also of the list of present members herewith sent.

" Master.
Senr. Warden.
Junr. Warden."

At a Lodge meeting held on the 22d December 1737, the charter of the Grand Lodge to the St

¹⁷³⁷ John's Inverness Masons was read, and ordained to be recorded in the Lodge's books for preservation. This important document runs as follows :—

" To all and sundry to whom these presents shall come, greeting, know yee, that wee, George, Earle of Cromarty, Lord Viscount of Tarbat, present Grand Master of the Grand Lodge of Free and Accepted Massons for the Kingdome of Scotland: Whereas, upon application to the Grand Lodge, in name of the Right Worshipful George Cuthbert of Castlehill, Esqr., present Master; John Mack Bean, Sherriff-Clerk of Inverness, Deputy-Master; John Dunbar, wryter in Inverness, Senr. Warden; and William Robertson, younger of Inshes, Worshipful Bretheren Free and Accepted Massons of the Lodge entituled Old Inverness Kilwinning, for themselves, and in name and behalf of the other Brethren belonging to the said Lodge, it was evidently made appear to us and our Brethren of the Grand Lodge, by proper documents, that from the twenty-seventh of December, one thousand six hundred and seventy-eight, they have been constituted and erected in a regular Masson Lodge by the name and designation of Old Inverness Kilwinning aforsaid, since which time they have been in use to keep regular meetings in which they have received and entered apprentices, past ffellow crafts, and raised Master Massons, and for that purpose have keept regular books, wherein they entred their proceedings in the way and manner practised in other well govern'd Masson's Lodges, and, as such, stand recorded in the books of the Grand Lodge; and wherein, by their representatives, they have been in use to vote at all the proceedings

of the same since the twelfth of October last bypast, 1737
as appears by the books and minutes of the Grand
Lodge of that date; and the Brethren aforsaid being
now desirous to have their forsaid erection and constitution ratified and confirmed by the Grand Lodge,
and for that end to have a Charter thereof in these
termes made out in their favours: Therefore, witt ye
us, with the advyce and consent of our Brethren of
the Grand Lodge, to have ratified, approven, and
confirmed, and by the tenor hereof, with consent forsaid, ratify, approve, and perpetually confirm the
aforsaid erection and constitution in favours of the
saids Worshipfull Brethren of Old Inverness Kilwinning, and their successors, and of new to have
constituted, erected, and appointed, and hereby erect,
constitute, and appoint them and their successors a
true and regular Lodge of Free and Accepted Massons
under the title and designation as mentioned, in all
time comeing, and ordain all the regular Masson
Lodges in Scotland to hold and respect them as such
for the future, hereby giveing, granting, and committing to them and their successors full and ample
power to meet as a regular Lodge, receive and enter
apprentices, pass fellow crafts, and raise Master
Masons, upon payment of regular and reasonable
compositions for supporting their poor decayed
brethren, widows, and orphans, agreeable to their
stations, and to elect and make choice of Masters,
Wardens, Thesaurers, and other office-bearers annually, or other ways as they shall have occasion;
and wee hereby, with consent forsaid, enjoyne and
recomend the said brethren to reverence and obey
their superiours in all things lawfull and honest, as
becomes the honour and harmony of Masonry in

generall; and shall faithfully become bound and engaged not to desert their Lodge, and that none of them presume, upon any pretence whatsomever, to make any separate or schismaticall meetings among themselves without the consent, approbation, and presence of their Master and Wardens for the time, nor shall they collect money or other separate fund from the common stock of their Lodge, to the hurt and detriment of their poor thereof, the said Worshipfull Brethren being always bound and obliged, as by their acceptation hereof, they faithfully bind and oblige them and their successors in all time comeing, to obtemper faithfully and obey the whole acts, statutes, and regulations of the Grand Lodge, their superiours, as well as those already made, as those hereafter to be made for the utility and prosperity of Masonry in generall, and to pay and performe whatever is or shall be stipulated and demanded from them for support of the Grand Lodge, and shall record in their books this present Charter, with the regulations hereafter to be made by them from time to time, to the effect the same may be more readily seen and observed by their Brethren, subject, nevertheless, to the review, and under correction of the Grand Lodge; and in like manner the aforsaid Brethren are hereby appointed and required punctually to attend the whole generall meetings and quarterly communications of the Grand Lodge, as they shall be advised thereof by their representatives, being their Master and Senior and Junior Wardens for the time, or by proxies in their places, duly authorized by commission from their Lodge: Provideing the said proxies be to Master Massons or ffellow crafts belonging to some establisht Lodge, to

the end the Brethren aforsaid may then act and vote
in the affairs of the Grand Lodge, and may be duely
certiorate and apprysed of the whole proceedings
thereof, and to whom they may represent yr. griev-
ances from time to time, as they shall see cause:
Declareing the aforsaid Brethren their precedency in
the Grand Lodge to be and commence from the aforsaid twenty-seventh of December, one thousand six
hundred and seventy-eight years, in respect ane extract of their erection was of that date produced and
openly read in the Grand Lodge; and to the effect
these presents may be the more effectually keept and
preserved, wee, with consent forsaid, appoint the
same to be recorded in the books of the said Grand
Lodge, in termes of the regulations made thereannent.
In witness whereof these presents are written by
Archibald Kennedy, writer in Edinburgh, Depute-
Clerk of the said Grand Lodge, and given under our
hand in the Grand Lodge held in Mary's Chappell in
Edinburgh this thirtieth day of November, one thou-
sand seven hundred and thirty-seven years, being the
date of our election, in presence of William Congal-
toun, your. of that ilk, Esq.; Charles Alston, Esq.,
Doctor of Medicine, our Senior and Junior Grand
Wardens; John M'Dougal, Grand Secretary; Major
John Robertson of Earnock, present Master of the
Lodge of Hamilton; Archibald Gowan, writer in
Edinburgh, present Master of the Lodge of Greenock
Kilwinning; and Archibald Kennedy, as designed,
present Master of the Lodge of Maybole; and George
Fraser, Esq., Deputy-Auditor of Excise, late Right
Worshipfull Master of the Lodge of Cannongate Kil-
winning. So signed, Cromartie, G.M.; Will. Con-
galton, S.G.W.; Charles Alston, J.G.W.; J. M'Dou-

gall, G. Secretary; J. Robertson, Hamilton Kilwinning, witnes; Archd. Govane, Greenock Kilwinning,
witnes; Geo. Frazer, witnes; Archd. Kennedy,
Maybole, witnes."

Follows the docquet—"Subscryved by the Grand
Clerk on the back of the forsaid Charter, bearing its
haveing been registered in the books of the Grand
Lodge," which is thus—

"Grand Lodge, 30th November 1737.
"Then the within Patent was recorded in the
books of the Grand Lodge in terms of the Regulations thereanent, by me, Clerk to, and Keeper of,
the said Record, so signed,
"R. ALISONE, Gr. Clerk."

The original Charter, though much mutilated, is
still preserved.

At a meeting held on the 27th December 1737,
a list of all the Brethren belonging to the Lodge was
enrolled in the minutes, and the arrears [of quarter
pennies] due to the Lodge, "*according to the old
Book.*" From this list it appears that the members
of the Lodge were in all 55—being masters, 19;
fellow crafts, 10; and entered apprentices, 26. I may
mention some of the more prominent names—

George Cuthbert of Castlehill.
John M'Bean, Sheriff-Clerk of Inverness.
Captain John Robertson.
Duncan Fraser, merchant.
Archibald Grahame, officer of Excyse.
William Robertson, younger of Inches.

Robert Whittingdale, teacher of the mathematicks. [1737]

John Baillie, writer to the Signet.

Charles Falconer, wryter.

James Thomson, Admirall Macer (?).

Robert Edward, music. master.

James Cuthbert, messenger.

William Kerr, officer of Excyse.

Hector Scott of Sandiland.

Farquhar M'Gillivray of Dunmaglass.

John Matheson, musician (his quarter pence "pd. by musick.")

Donald M'Bean of Phaillie.

Mr John Forrester, late Sheriff-Clerk of Invss.

Hugh Mackay, son to Clashmach.

The following were admitted shortly after the preceding list was made up :—

James Mackintosh of Morrill.

Donald M'Gillivray of Dalcromby.

William Shaw of Craigfield.

John Mackintosh of Culclachy.

Lachlan M'Bean, glover, and brother to John M'Bean, Sheriff-Clerk of Inverness.

Gillies MackBean, tacksman of Bonnachton.

Robert M'Pherson, tacksman of Pyperhill.

James Dallas of Cantray.

Andrew Rose, officer of Excyse.

Charles M'Lean, merchant at Fort-Augustus.

Alexr. Simson, *alias* Fraser, in Castlehill.

Mr William Grant, schoolmaster there.

On the 9th January 1738, it was resolved, " That,.

in regard the Lodge and Brotherhood are soe numerous as that there is noe need of admitting many more, and considering that the communicating the secrets of the Lodge to too many persons would be unworthy," not to increase the numbers without the unanimous consent of all the members present at the quarterly meetings.

At the same time it was enacted that "if at any time, while the Lodge is open, and the Brethren employed about their public business, any brother or fellow craft shall swear or curse, he shall be decerned and amerciate to pay six shillings Scots money for each oath and transgression; and that if any brother shall aggrage the said crime by the frequent and reiterated commission of it, that in that case the punishment may be augmented and proportioned to the crime by the majority of voices of the fraternity."

Fines were also exacted for absence of any brother without leave. These fines seem to have been rigorously enforced throughout the existence of the Lodge till the present day ; but I regret to say a laxity now exists on this point.

The Lodge seems to have possessed an interest Trades Houses, &c. in the property and lands along with the Six Incorporated Trades of Inverness; and from time to time these rents were divided, and the Freemasons received their share. On the 16th of June 1738, they instruct—"That Alexr. Fraser, Thesaurer, Doe forthwith and without loss of time prosecute the action before the Sherriff depending against the incorporate Trades to a finall sentence, as also all the other debtors of the Lodge." By the minutes of 26th March 1739, we learn that the Lodge possessed a seventh share in the rents of the Trades lands.

On the 20th April 1739, Alexander Drummond, 1739
Provincial Grand Master of Scotland, visited the
Lodge, and, on being "entreated," took the chair,
and "lectured the brethren for their instruction."
Thereafter the healths of the office-bearers of the
Grand Lodge were drunk, "and the ordinary songs
sung." This Alexander was the first appointed
Provincial Grand Master, and his district was pro-
perly of the lodges in the western counties. The
erection of the Moray district followed in 1747,
John Baillie, Esq., W.S., being P.G.M.; the next,
1756, Sir Wm. Dunbar of Westfield, and in 1801
James Brodie of Brodie, who was succeeded by his
son in 1827.

On the 25th June 1739, the brethren resolved to
lend Brother Nicolson £4 to carry on a law plea in
defence of his just rights. The minute is as follows:

"It was moved by Brother Falconar by proxie Brotherly
by Brother Nicolson, that as the fundamentale de-help.
sign and purpose of gathering a publick fund in this
and all other lodges must be interpreted principally
to be for the support of Brethren in indigent
necessities, and as the said Brother Nicolson is immediately imbarrassed with a plea in defence of his
just right and property in ane heritage in this
burgh, before the Lords of Session, by one John
Grant, vexatiously: And as Brother Nicolson wants
cash to support his plea, and is still willing to give
heritable security for four pound sterling, to be
borrowed for support of his plea: That therefore
the question should be put and the vote stated to
each individual member of the quarterly communication whether or not the said Brother Nicolson

2

should have the said loan, and the question being
accordingly put, and the vote stated, it was appointed at the sight of the master or deputy-master,
and any two or more of the members of the Lodge
being master masons, to give four pound sterling to
the said John Nicolson, and take the security therefore."

Contribu-
tion to Edin-
burgh Infir-
mary.

In September 1739 a circular was received from
the Grand Lodge, requesting the St John's Lodge to
contribute towards the £100 promised by the Grand
Lodge as a subscription to the Edinburgh Infirmary,
and the Lodge responded by promising a contribution of £5. 5s. On the 5th March 1740 £1. 1s. was
remitted, being the "first two moyeties of the quota
determined on." So well did the Freemasons throughout Scotland respond to this charitable appeal that
the directors intimated their intention that preference should always be given to Freemasons in one of
the galleries of the Royal Infirmary.

The first proxy appointed to represent St John's
Lodge in Edinburgh was John Baillie, Writer to the
Signet, on 3d November 1739.

Good
behaviour
enjoined.

Precautions against drunkenness seem to have
been considered necessary, as on 15th November
1739, we find it enacted—

"That any Brother coming to the Lodge drunk
or taken with liquor shall be put to the award and
amerciate in one shilling sterling for the first offence,
and in two shillings sterling for the second, and for
the third to be turned out of the Lodge untill he is
received upon his solemn recantation and payment of
his amerciament, at the discretion of the Lodge.

"GEO. CUTHBERT, Mr."

About this time the Brethren, after negotiating with the Six Incorporated Trades as to the Lodge's title and share in their mortcloath, resolved upon "the buying of a handsome mortcloath for the benefits of the Lodge," and on the 5th March 1740 the committee appointed to meet with Bailie Thomas Alves, in order to commission a mortcloth. Accordingly, upon the 4th day of February they did "meet with the said Bailie Alves, and in name of the whole Lodge did commission him to send to Holland for ten yeards of Genoua velvet, ten yeards of sairge lining, four pound of Baladyn silk, with as much glazed lining as was sufficient to go betwixt the velvet and lining; they obliging themselves to receive the same at his hands upon a moderat profit, he runing all sea hazards and other risques, the value of which they obliged themselves to pay in three months after the receipt thereof,"—of which transaction the Lodge generally approved.

This mortcloth seems to have been of considerable importance in the eyes of the Brethren, and we find that on the arrival of the materials from Holland they were "viewed."

On the 25th June 1740, "The Lodge being informed that Mr Thomas Alves, Mercht. in Inverness, having received the velvet, &c., commissioned by the Lodge for a mortcloath the fourth of Febry. last, doe appoint the Master and late Master, two Wardens, Duncan Fraser, John Nicolson, John Dunbar, Alexr. Fraser, and the present Theasurer to wait of Mr Alves upon Fryday, the 27th curt., in order to receive the said velvet, &c., and to give proper security for the same in name of the Lodge, according to the Act of the 25th March last, and upon receipt thereof, to deliver the said velvet, &c., to Alexander Clark, taylor in Inverness, in order to be made into a mort-cloath for the use of the said Lodge."

Having given orders for payment of the cost of the mortcloth to Mr Alves, amounting to £19, and counted their funds, the Lodge called on the whole Brethren present (1st October 1740) and in arrear to the Lodge, who were "publicly advertis'd, that as horning was already expede and execute agst. them upon a decreet before the Sheriff of Inverness, that such as did not clear their foresaid debt betwixt and the third current hade only themselves to blame for future deligence, the Lodge being fully resolved, and have given particular orders to the Theasurer to put the sd. horning upon the fourth current for caption, and yt. the sd. caption will be put in execution without loss of time."

On the same day the Master appointed a committee of six members "to meet and inspect the frenges and oyr. furniture belonging to the mortcloath made by Duncan M'Queen's wife; and, if need bees, to call for oyr. people skilled in such commodities to take their approbation of the same, and according to the sufficiency of the said work, to determine the price thereof, for which the Lodge hes given them power; and lykeways ordains the said comittee to inspect the frenge in the hands of one James Fraser, whether it be fit for the small mortcloth."

At a meeting on the 12th December 1740, it was moved that "a just & regular list of Brethrene, having title to and property of the two mortcloaths now finished and in our possession, be forthwith engrossed at the end of the Book of By-laws. That others hereafter entering apprentices to this Lodge, and paying a certain sume to be hereafter mentioned, may have there names added yrto."

"The question being put, the Lodge unanimously agree thereto, and ordains the same to pass into an Act as follows, viz.:—That in regard the primitive designe of procuring a mortcloath for the Lodge was no other than to have it in our power to see indigent Brethren decently and honourably interrd: But as the saids mortcloath are subject to wear, it is hereby enacted that each entred apprentice, after the date hereof, shall imediately pay in to the Thesaurer the sume of ffour pounds Scots money for the suport of the saids mortcloaths, each member payeing the above sume, or having title as above, shall not only have the benefit of the saids mortcloaths for himself, but also for his wife and children, during their stay in his family. It is further enacted that all operative brethren, that can not show proper vouchers for their having satisfied the Thesaurer for the time being of them paying to the said Thesaurer the forsaid sume of ffour pounds Scots for their benefite of the trades mortcloath, as the same is found to be an infringement upon the property of others of operative bretheren that have paid the same, as the money arising from the sale of the saids trads mortcloath was apply'd to the purchasing of the sd., and they ordain that this act be transferred to page seventeen of the Book of By Laws, under which act a regular list of members, having title to the saids cloaths, are ordained to be registrate from time to time. It is further enacted—That all freemen's children, hereafter entering into this Lodge, shall pay the sume of one pound ten shillings Scots moe. for their priviledge to the sd. cloaths."

On the 15th December 1741 an entry occurs— "Angus M'Intosh, *youngest* merchant in Inverness, was admitted to the liberties of our mortcloaths."

So far as can be ascertained, there existed a jealousy on the part of the operative members of St John's Lodge against the superior social position of the members of the junior Lodge. The gentlemen belonging to the former, having but few of their own equals within it, were apt, in their seasons of conviviality, to prefer the society of the members of the sister Lodge, which was composed of the elite of the town and neighbourhood. This gave great offence to the operative members, and in retaliation they resorted to an unusual step.

On the 17th December 1740, after the election of the office-bearers had taken place, after the Lodge had been "decently and orderly shut," and the minutes authenticated by the signature of " Dun. Fraser, Mr," some ten of the members met and reopened the Lodge, and " continued at the annuall communication." Headed by Charles Falconar (wryter), who had just been elected Senior Warden, as " Chairman in place of the ' Master,' " they passed the following resolution :—

" It was enacted that in respect the Master, Duncan Fraser, and George Cuthbert, Brother, have withdrawn themselves this day from the Lodge, being St John's Day, and that after dining with the Brethren and crave joyned their Sister Lodge (notwithstanding the Master and Brother Cuthbert were in a brotherly way severall times sent for, and that the Master, upon his appearance, acknowledged that he was bound to attend another societie, and that he

would not attend the Brethren of his own Lodge) the
said Duncan Fraser and George Cuthbert be amerciate as follows, viz., the said Duncan Fraser, Master,
in the sum of ten shillings and sixpence sterling, and
the said George Cuthbert in the sum of five shillings
moie. forsd., to be applied towards the publick good,
and payed in to the Treasurer of the Lodge against
the next meeting."

This minute is signed by the members approving
of the resolution. The first is "Charles Falconar,"
who adds to his signature, "This was done by
plurality of voices of the Brethren," and nine names
follow, two of the members, Robert Sim and Alexander Fraser, using Roman letters as their "mark,"
being apparently unable to write. It is worthy of
note that William Robertson, younger of Iuches, was
present at this meeting, but neither he nor John
Dunbar, who was Secretary to the Lodge, append
their signatures to the resolution, and would seem to
be the dissentients alluded to in Brother Falconar's
note.

At the next meeting, held on 28th January 1741,
"but a few in number of the Lodge present, and
that Castlehill as well as Duncan Fraser is denounced
by the above Act, and that Castlehill is absent, the
entering on the said Act is deferred till a full meeting," and the matter is referred to the cognisance
and determination of a committee.

On the 2d February the Committee report to the
Lodge :—

"The Comitee appointed to cognosce in the affair
in relation to the Master and George Cuthbert of

1741   Castlehill being fined by a sentence of the Senior
Warden, 27th Decr. last, the said Comittee, Archibald
Grahame, Deputy Master, yrin presiding, have given
in there oppinion in manner following, vizt.—That
in regaird the Senior Warden opened the Lodge the
27th December last, after nyne o'clock at night, and
after the Lodge was orderly shut by the master and
the business of the day finished, and the Deputy
Master retyred to his lodging: It thereby appears
the said Warden had no other than a view in the
raising sedition, by taking upon him to open a Lodge
at an unseasonable tyme of night, when the proper
officers legally authorized to exercise that office were
retyred, and by pretending to impose an Act of his
own composing without the sanction of the Lodge,
which pretended Act the Comittee this day conveened doe annul and make void to all intents and
purposes, which sentence of the said Comittee is by
the genll. consent yrof signed by

              " ARCHD. GRAHAME, D.-Mr."

The preceding extracts relating to this affair
were engrossed on the pages following page 19 of the
minute-book, which pages were immediately afterwards pasted together, for on the 29th Septr. 1741,
George Cuthbert of Castlehill, late Master, enters a
protest against such practices in the following vigorous manner—

" Eodem die, George Cuthbert of Castlehill, one
of the Members and late Master, haveing been at
this communication and necessarily absent from the
two former communications since the annual meeting,
finds—That by reviseing the Register of our Lodge

since that time there have been abuses committed, particularly by bathring the two leaves preceding this, wherein a great many Acts relating to the private affairs of our Lodge and otherwayes have thereby been destroyed, I, the said George Cuthbert of Castlehill, doe hereby protest that all acts and deeds done or signed since that time shall be void and null, and never militate against me the said George, by the subsequent acts, and also that I require as Member of the said Lodge, that all the pages from this present page shall be numbered, this being the twenty-third, and I also protest that the Right Worshipfull Master, and all the whole Members present, shall condemn and hereby uterly abhorr such practices as aforsaid; upon which the said George Cuthbert took instruments in the hands of me, John Dunbar, Secretary to the said Lodge.

(Signed) "GEO. CUTHBERT."

It is curious that the page whereon this vigorous protest is recorded, though styled 23d, is numbered 21; the first number was correct, but the "bathring" of the two pages made it actually 21. I may add that although some previous attempts seem to have been made to detach these leaves, it was not, from the time when Castlehill denounced the act in 1741, till the other day, that the minutes referred to were brought to light.

Returning to the "dining out" question, we find at the meeting on 8th April 1741—Duncan Fraser, merchant, Inverness, Master—"It was moved by all the Brethren present except the Master,—That the haill brethren be certiorate that againe the twenty-fourth June next, being the immediat succeeding

1741   quarterly communication, the question is to be put, to be determined by the plural voice of the brotherhood, whether or not any brother of this Lodge, after the shutting of the Lodge upon the annual communication day, may immediately thereafter goe and leave the Brethren, and communicat or conferr with our Sister Lodge without libertie had of the Brethren by the plurall voices by balls or otherwayes."

Accordingly, on the 24th June, " In consequence of the last act, the question was put and it was unanimously voted by the haill Brethren present and enacted—That non of the Brethren doe without leave askt and obtained of the Brotherhood leave the Lodge on the anuall communication day and goe and communicate with our Sister Lodge by balling, dancing, drinking, or otherwise, under the penalty of ten shillings and sixpence sterling for Master, Wardens or other office-bearers in the Lodge, and ffive shillings sterling for each brother that shall presume to contravene this act, to be payed into the black box as oft as they shall transgress."

But the matter did not end here. In the last minute the operative members seem to have carried their views. The other party, although acquiescing in the resolution, yet resolve to punish the chief actor in the quarrel, Charles Falconar, writer, and on the 29th of September, Archibald Grahame, "officer of excyse," late Master, gave in a complaint, signed by him, against Charles Falconar; which was referred to a Committee directed to meet upon the 29th of October, and the Tyler "is immediately ordered to deliver the said Charles Falconar a double of the charge, and suite him to appear againe the day forsaid and place where he is to be charged."

The delinquent, however, did not attend to the summons of the Committee, for on the 1st of December "Archibald Grahame presented and insisted upon his deliverance on his Memoriall above mentioned against Charles Falconar, and in regaird he did not appear, although twice personally cited, being in a neighbouring room in the same house—the Lodge unanimously agreed that he should be cited to the 15th current, in order to give in his answers to the Memoriall given against him, and of which he has a double in his custodie these sex weeks past, with certification that if he does not appear againe the above day, to give in his answers, that he will be excluded the Lodge, and this the Secretary of the Lodge is ordered to intimate the same to him that he may not pretend ignorance."

On the 15th December "The complaint of Archibald Grahame against Charles Falconar is continued till St John's Day ensuing."

It was not till the 25th of June 1742—eighteen months from the commencement of the quarrel—that it was at length amicably settled. On that day "compeared Brethren Grahame and Falconar, who in present of the Master, Lodge, and Brethren loveingly accorded all differences formerly subsisting betwixt them, and in token of a full reconciliation, kissed each other three times, and gave their promise of good behaviour and amitie to each other in the future, in presence of the Master and Brethren convocated on this meeting." And afterwards "it is enacted that any Brethren discording, soe as by willful absence of either of them, or otherwise disonering the Lodge by breaking the harmonie thereof, shall stand to be advised and suffer such pains and penalties as the Master and Brotherhood shall please inflict on the offenders."

I have given the details of this episode in the history of our Lodge at some length, as it seems to have excited strong feelings during its progress, is amusing in itself, and illustrative of the manners of the period. The Duncan Fraser so often mentioned was of the family of Achnagairn, merchant, and afterwards Provost of Inverness, who was so harshly treated by orders of the Duke of Cumberland for interposing in favour of the wounded prisoners taken at Culloden. He occupied the house, or one on the same site as the house in Church Street now used as the Parochial Board offices. John Dunbar was a member of a family of merchants who were for a long period connected with Inverness. They were wealthy and munificent benefactors to the burgh. George Cuthbert of Castlehill was Sheriff-Depute of Inverness-shire, under Simon, Lord Lovat. He was said to have been a great persecutor of witches, and he met his death in the year 1748 by a fall from his horse at the eastern extremity of the vale of Aultmournach. This is the valley leading from Culcabock to the Aberdeen Road, long famous as a resort of the fairies and kindred spirits, who were popularly supposed to have caused his death in this locality.

I will now resume my running commentary on, and extracts from, the minutes.

Lax attend-
ance of
Members. The attendance having been somewhat lax, the following resolution was enacted on the 31st March 1742:—

"The Lodge having observed for some years past that severalls of the Brethren, in contempt of the

salutary laws and regulations of this Lodge, have 1742
wilfully absented themselves from their quarterly
communications, and thereby putting the Brethreen,
who doe attend into an unreasonable expence in
mentaining the honour and dignity of the Lodge,
and that after repeated admonishments given each of
them to give more punctual attention for the futtur,
which they have hitherto contemed to their great
dishonor; therefore the Mr. and Brethren present at
this quarterly communication, having seriously taken
the same into consideration, have agreed, nemine
contradicente, that any brother absenting himself
from any of the quarterly communications yrof for
the futtur, without giving a satisfactory reason
yrfore, to be delivered personally, sent in wryting,
or sent by a broyr., to the Lodge, and the verity of
qlk must be so clearly vouched, as must be satisfactory to the sd. Lodge, that nothing but plane matters
of fact is mean'd thereby, with certification to the
contraveeners thereof, yt upon his being convict of
such contempt, hie shall from the moment of such
conviction be deprived of all benefits and immunitys
of the Lodge, such as the benefit of the mortcloaths,
and ye subsystence given indigent Brethren, &c., for
all time comeing, and their names canceld from the
list of those yt have the benefits yrof, and they
ordein a duplicate of this to be extracted from the
records, to be promulgate to each member of this
Lodge, betwixt and the 24 June next, being the
next quarterly communication, yt non may pretend
ignorance."

It is probable that this censure was directed
against the absentees and frequenters of the Sister

1742   Lodge, as it was promulgated during the period of the discords just related. It is curious to note what in the estimation of the members was the heaviest punishment that could be inflicted upon the offenders, viz., deprivation of the "benefits of the mortcloaths." It exemplifies a worthy trait in the Scottish character, that of providing for oneself and friends a decent and orderly burial, and seems also to indicate that "a mortcloath" was an article not yet provided by private enterprise, but like many another in that age could be procured only by a close corporation for its own members. Union of affinities was *then* the ruling principle; *now*, it is each for himself; and notwithstanding our boasted progress, it is doubtful which is the better of the two. There can be none as to which is the kindliest.

Masonic Processions

At this time Lodge processions were conducted with great regularity and much pomp. On every St John's Day the Masons walked, properly clothed, through the streets of the town. The meetings for business commenced often as early as nine o'clock A.M. On the occasion of the annual election of office-bearers, the Lodge walked thereafter in procession to church, in communion with the other Lodges.

The Mort-cloth.

The possession of the mortcloth by the Lodge seems to have been regarded with some pride, and a participation in its "benefits" a matter of great importance in the eyes of the Brethren. It occupies a very considerable amount of attention, and references to it frequently occur by which we may form some idea of the esteem with which it was regarded. Thus, on 15th December 1742, it "was complained of by severalls of the Brethren that their names was not inrolled in the list of members that had priviledge to the mortcloaths, . . . and disputes having risen among the Brethren, and objections being made by some of them agt. the complainers being inrolled in the list, . . . the question was stated—Whether or not all the free members of this Lodge, at the date when the mortcloaths were . . . delivered, &c., which was the 12th December 1740, . . . ought to be free to the priviledges of the same, and the question being put akordingly, it carried fourteen to sex in the affirmative."

It was further enacted that all entrants to the Lodge, on payment of £4 Scots beyond the regular dues of entrance, should have the said priviledge; the sons of members to acquire the same on payment of "ane half crown." Hereon follows a protest by certain of the members, and a lengthy minute recording the arguments adduced on either side—styled "complainers" and "protesters." The former, who were the majority, remind their opponents "that they might charge the protesters . . . to account for their administration . . . of the publick money of the Lodge for thirty years preceding the making up the Lodge's mortcloaths, and for which publick money ther is non heard of or accounted for but these tryfells payed in to the trades mortcloath." They are, however, too magnanimous to do so: unanimously object to "any retrospeck" at all, and intreat their brethren to depart from their protest, "and cordially agree with the plural voice of the brethren as becometh."

Again, on 27th December following, we find the mortcloth referred to :—

"The Lodge unanimously aggreed that Alexr.

1742   Fraser, late Junior Warden, should keep the mortcloaths for the ensuing year—he obliging himself to
keep the same free of all damage, as he shall answer
therefor to the Lodge, and they ordain a quorum to
inspect the said cloaths now in the possession of
Donald Fraser, and to make their report thereof before the same is delivered to Alexr. Fraser."

The Minutes   It may be here observed that the minutes of this
period were carefully attested by the Master.   They
appear to have been engrossed during the meeting,
and each subject or matter disposed of was separately
signed by the Master, the following business being
introduced by the words, "Eodem die," or "Ther-
after."

Discipline.   The records of the year 1743 are crowded with
cases of "discipline," and the conduct of many of the
members brought upon them the censure of the
Lodge.   On the 25th March, a peculiar phrase is
introduced, "The Master and Brethren finding that
severalls of the Brethren that were to be delated for
irregularity in their conduct as Masons, had *indus-
triously* absconded from this communication day,"
adjourn the meeting till the 31st, when the Tyler
is ordered to summon the offenders."

Accordingly on that day :—

Robert   "Robert Nicolson having been accused last quar-
Nicolson,   terly communication day for entering ane apprentice
of his, and allowing him to congregate with a neighbouring Lodge without the advice and consent of the
Master, &c., of this Lodge, who being legally cited
to this dyet, and not compearing, tho' sent for, refers any progress therein until next quarterly day.

Thereafter, John Tulloch was put to the award by 1743
Brothers Falconar and Dunbar for acting in conjunction with some strolling brethren in entring
Rodrick M'Leod without any dispensation from this
Lodge so to do. But in regard that the said Tulloch
appears to be noways affected for such an offence,
nor can be calmed by the most brotherly admonition,
therefore referrs the determination of this case to the
next quarterly day, after seriously reminding him to
think more coolly of this his offence, as the same is
deometrically opposite to the laudable laws and regulations of this Lodge; that upon his repentance and
serious acknowledgment and recantation, he may be
not only brought to a true sense of his fault in giving
offence to the Brotherhood, but learn how to prevent
the like in time coming, by liveing in that harmony
becoming fellows of such a society."

On the 28th of June, the Lodge having considered
the " accusation and complaint against Robert Nicolson, he having appeared at this present meeting, and
the same being read in his presence, and he being
required to give his answers thereto, he, the said
Robert Nicolson, denied the whole facts sett forth
against him therein: To which it is answered by
John Dunbar, member of this Lodge, and in name and
behalf of Charles Falconar and severall other members of this Lodge, that he and they will prove the
accusation and complaint as sett forth as aforesaid,
and particularly that they will prove that he was
present at the entering of his own apprentice, or
was accessory thereto, sometime summer last, in or
about John Clark's house, or some other house,
in the lands called Pettie. The Lodge, considering

3

1743   what has been said on both sides, and finding their
number too few at this time, referrs the consideration
of the premises to the next quarterly communication,
and ordains John Dunbar, and the rest who concurs
with him, to adduce a proof again that day.

"And in regaird that John Tulloch (also put to
the award by the former sederunt) is absent, notwithstanding that he was regularly summoned to
attend this meeting, and he contemptuously (for
ought the Lodge knows) disregarding the same. The
Lodge condemns him to the award, and fined in Two
Pounds Scots, he being personally present this day
in town.

"And it has been further complained by Archd.
Grahame, Senior Warden, that upon the date of the
former sederunt, when he presided in absence of the
Master, that upon his sending the Boxmaster and
Tailor to the house of Robert Nicolson and oyrs.
absent that day, with power to them (according to
the laudable custom of this Lodge) in case they did
not willingly come to attend the Lodge, to bring a
poind equall in value to the fine instituted by this
Lodge in the by-laws, the other members either being
from home or comeing to give attendance with all
due submission; Robert Nicolson complained off
absolutely deneyed either to give presence or a poind,
and told the sd. Boxmaster, &c., that if the said
Archibald Grahame wou'd order a poind from him
that he knew how to be redressed by the civill law.
The said being putt to him, the said Robert Nicolson, he acknowledges the facts, but did not esteem
them criminall. The Lodge having considered Mr
Grahame's complaint agt. Robert Nicolson, in regaird of the reasons aforesaid, viz., the paucity of

our number, continues the consideration of the fore- 1743
said complaint to the next quarterly communication,
being the 29th of September next, and recommends
Brother Nicolson to think of his duty to the Lodge
of which he is a member betwixt and that time."

After so lengthy a minute, recording such heinous Respect for
the Church
crimes and misdemeanours, the conclusion is most and Clergy. .
lame and impotent. On the 29th of September the
attendance was so small that no Lodge was held, and
on the next Lodge day, on the 22d of November, the
articles against Brothers Nicolson and Tulloch were
again referred to the succeeding communication, on
account of the Master's absence. The affair is finally
disposed of on the 17th of January 1744, when
"Brother Robert Nicolson compeared; after reading
the award, with the letter he sent last St John's Day,
to the Lodge, he was advised, in the most brotherly
manner, to consider the consequences of such, which
he did by a humble submission to the Lodge's desire,
and was accordingly received into the favor of all
the brotherhood." Another and more edifying pic-
ture of the manners of the period is exhibited in the
respect shown for the ordinances and the ministers
of religion. The several Lodges in the town annually
upon St John's Day, in December, met together and
went in procession to the church. On the 27th of
December 1741, the Rev. Alexander Macbean, who
was a member of the St Andrew Lodge, had preached
a sermon which met the approval of the Masons, for
on the 28th of June 1743 we read—

"The Lodge having taken into consideration the
most excellent sermon preached by the Rev. Alex-

1743 ander Macbean, minister of the Gospel here, upon
the 27th December 1741, the same has been pub-
lished at the desire of several Lodges of free and accepted Masons, Wee doe hereby ordain that fifty
coppies of said sermon shall be taken into this Lodge,
and the Lodge orders Donald Fraser, present generall
boxmaster to the trades of Inverness, to pay to the
said Mr Alexr. Macbean the sum of two pounds ten
shillings sterline out off the rents of the Trades
House arising from the seventh part of the rents of
the said house, belonging to the Free Masons of this
Lodge . . . . and wee doe hereby ordain that the
coppies shall be lodged in the box, and the boxkeeper
is hereby ordered to give a coppie to each member,
they granting receipt therefore, and wee desire this
our act to be forthwith intimated to the Reverend
Mr M'Bean by Donald Fraser, and that Donald
Fraser receive the coppies as said is."

Again, on the 22d November following—

"There were severall coppies of Mr MackBean's
sermon (now depositate in the hands of our Junior
Warden and Lodgekeeper) distribute to the members
present . . . . and ordained him to deliver to the
absent brethren each a coppie when required."

On the 16th of December "the Lodge unanimously resolved to make their procession to the
church in communion with our Sister Lodge, and
ordain all members to be charged to attend the Lodge
that day betwixt the hours of eight and nine in the
morning."

The Rev. Alexr. MacBean, A.M., here referred

to, whose sermon afforded such gratification to the 1743
brethren, was for forty-two years a minister in Inverness, much loved and respected by the inhabitants.
He was called from Douglas on the 16th February
1720 to the Gaelic Church, translated to the second,
and afterwards to the first charge, and died in the
year 1762.

The proprietors in the neighbourhood and the
gentry of the town seem to have rather affected St
Andrew's Lodge than the present Lodge of St John,
though occasionally some of their names appear among
the entrants into this Lodge.

The Brethren seem to have been somewhat per-Book-keep-
ing and
plexed by the manner in which their Treasurers or Finance.
Boxmasters kept an account of their intromissions,
and the following minute lays down rules for their
guidance:—

"17 January 1744.—The Lodge unanimously 1744
aggreed that ane opening in the mark book be
draughted [ruled] for keeping ane accompt of what
money may after the date hereof arise to the benefite
of the mortcloaths by entred prentices, &c., and that
such mony shall, at every Lodge day after the receipt
thereof, be putt into a purse now lying in the box,
with a note on paper of the quantity then putt in,
and so repeated on every occasion of the like nature,
which money, thus kept separately from any oyr. per-
quisites of the Lodge, shall be examined into every
meeting: that wee may be thorowly perswaded that
none thereof is imbazled, the better to enable us to
maintain the said mortcloath by purchassing ane oyr.
when this shall faill."

Not only the book-keeping but the conduct of their Boxmaster troubled the Lodge. On the 17th January, John Munro being Boxmaster, "the Lodge having appointed this day to examine into the Thesaurer's intromissions, and to take out a true list of what arrears were due to the Lodge by bill or otherwise, but the Thesaurer not appearing, ordained a committee to meet to-morrow at this place to get out a true state thereof, . . and *that they are to meet on the said Thesaurer's charges.*"

The minute of the following day is stern and brief—

"Inverness, 18th January 1744.—When the committee mett, and the Thesaurer not appearing, was, by the unanimous voice of the Lodge, fined in three merks Scots for the benefite of the poor, and ordains the same to be charged to his accompt."

On the 4th of February the Treasurer and the committee met and adjusted accounts. There was found due to the Lodge the sum of £1. 3s. 2d. sterling, "which he was ordered forthwith to depositate in the box as usuall, upon which he went off without giveing satisfaction."

At the Lodge held on 2d March following the Treasurer added to his offences—

"John Munro, Boxmaster, haveing in face of the Lodge contemptuously refused to pay four pounds Scots for his freedome to the mortcloath, . . . notwithstanding the Lodge offered their indulgence for five shillings he formerly promised for the use of said mortcloath to his mother, upon which his name was

cancelled from the list of members haveing title to 1744
said mortcloath; . . and they ordain that this shall
be minuted in their records for a memoriall against
him, as well as a precedent for others that shall for
the future show the like contempt, and ordains the
Senior Warden to prosecute the said John Monro
for the said five shillings."

These decided steps seem to have alarmed John,
for, on the 25th June, we read—

"John Monro, Boxmaster, haveing acknowledged
his fault in contemping of the autie. of the Lodge in
not attending their meetings when duly called for,
and in refusing to accept of the indulgence of the
former minute," he was again re-instated in the
favour of the Brethren, his fine of three merks Scots
remitted, as well as "the above five shillings, for
the use of the said mortcloath to his moyr., as the
Lodge is unwilling to use hard measures with a
brother that is known to his fault."

The Lodge took vigorous steps to recover arrears Arrears.
due by the members, and instructed their office-
bearers to recover the sums due by the process of
law. On the 2d of March, the amounts in arrear
having been fixed, the defaulters were directed before
the 7th to grant their "obligatory notes" for the
same, payable on the 26th; and the Lodge "ordains
those that faill to be set furth in the decreet to be
extracted that day." Accordingly, on the 26th
"none offering payment," the Lodge "ordains that
their several bills should be protested, and the decreet extracted against the remaining members be-

twixt and Fryday next, so that the same may be sent off to Edinr. for a horning thereon." On the 25th of June the several members in arrears by bills, and others decerned by decreet, were called to pay, but none appearing so to do, the Boxmaster and Secretary were directed to meet upon the 27th, when the former was to bring with him "all the bills in his custody not purged, as well as those that are : in order that ane horning may be sent for against them all upon Saturday, the 30th current." The patience of the Brethren was exhausted, as the minute concludes, "with certification as the last indulgence from the Lodge." However, on the 29th September, the Boxmaster having showed the bills protested, "but no money recovered," a further delay and another "*last* indulgence" was granted to the defaulters till the 18th of October, when he was instructed "to cause extract decreet agt. such as docs not comply wh. such indulgence."

The Lodge having incurred a debt to Alexander Clark, tailor, for the mortcloath, met on the 23d of November to consider as to its payment. The Boxmaster reports that he has in his hands £1. 10s. 8d., which, however, "wants 8 sh. to compleat" the sum due. The course resolved on was to draw a bill upon the Boxmaster at eight days after date, "drawn upon him this night, payable to ye said Alexr. Clark, in order"—the minute rather ungraciously adds—"that ye Lodge may be free of ye clamours of such a person."

Miscellaneous.

On the 25th June 1744, the Right Worshipful Master, Archibald Grahame, "delivered to the Lodge a very handsome Lecture upon Masonry, founded upon the originall principles thereof, vizt., Geometry,

Philosophy, and Divinity, with the original history of the said Noble Art of Masonry from the Creation to this present time, in the different periods, and concluded the same with very fine moral reflections upon the whole, and the Lodge unanimously returned him their hearty thanks, and the Lodge appoints their late Master to sign this Minute in their names, in testimony of their thanks."

Inverness was about this period, and for a considerable time after, the headquarters of two or three regiments. On the 14th December the first of the military Brethren was admitted, "Charles Ingram, Serjeant in Collonell Murray's Regiment of Foot," who "paid his compliment to the box with the ordinary treat to the Brotherhood." From this date the admission of soldiers was frequent.

The procession this year appears, from the allusions to it in the minutes, to have been rather more imposing than usual. On the 14th December the Lodge "resolved to meet by nine o'clock in the morning of St John's Day next at their hall, in order to prepair for their procession that forenoon," and the minute of that day records that they proceeded "through the streets of the town, according to ye ancient and laudable custom of this Lodge." The minute having been duly recorded and signed, the following note was appended to it:—

"N.B.—David Holland, present Master of the Lodge of Free Masons in the Honble. Brigadier Guise's Regt., now lying at Inverness, Fort-George, visited us this day, and had his proper place assigned him in our procession; he appears to be No. 45 Mrs. of the Lodge."

The meeting of 27th December is unequalled for the number of offenders whose delinquencies are recorded. Several of the country Brethren, viz., Cantray, Gillies M'Bean in Dalmagarry, and Donald M'Gilleray of Dalcrombie, are minuted as "still denying to pay their quarter pennies, and giveing proper attendance to the Lodge."

"And which is still worse, that Charles Falconar has been ane instrument in leading aside severalls of the town Brethren, viz., John M'Intosh of Culclachie, John Dunbar, Alexr. M'Intosh, Hector Scot, and Alexander Watson, and others, as haveing been at great pains to impose upon them to act contrary to the regulations and constitution of this Lodge, by innovating principles of his own and denying their personall presence. But also some of them by uttering things not to be mentioned in promiscuous companys, to the dishonour of the Lodge, with ane intent to make us contemptible in the eyes of the world. The Master therefor craved a vote of the Lodge, that it may be enacted that such should not be admitted as fellows of this Society, till they aither exculpate themselves of the grounds of this complaint, or come in under a sense of their misdemeanour betwixt and the twenty-fifth day of March next, and make a solemn recantation of their error and promise a better behaviour for the future. But in case they shall refuse to comply with this mild and brotherly admonished, that then they shall be holden as no member of this Lodge, and they immediately deprived of all immunities and priviledges thereof. And they ordain John Monro, the Boxmaster, to certifie each of them of the above."

On the 25th of March following none of the 1745
members, although all duly cited, put in an appearance. They were allowed till next quarterly communication—the 25th June—to give in answers to the
preceding charges, but fines for non-attendance, varying from 1s. 6d. to 2s. 6d., were imposed on no less
than eleven absentees.

The matter is not again alluded to; probably the
disturbed state of the country distracted the Brethren's thoughts from the investigation of matters of
gossip.

At the same meeting, on 25th March, the disor-
ganized and undisciplined state of the Lodge seems
to have been seriously considered. "The Mr. proposed that a conset set of charges, regulations, and
constitutions, &c., should be drawn up betwixt and
St John Baptist Day, that they may be regularly
engrossed in ye Book of Bye Laws for ye instruction
of young Brethren, and yt. each entred apprentice
may sign the same in testimony of his adherence to
them, and yt. his mark then taken out* may show
the members of this as well as oyr. Lodges the time
of his admission, &c., ye Lodge he belongs to, as well
as his age (in regaird that our charges we have in
force some years agoe when oyr. useless papers were
comitted to ye flames as is suposed by some of our
Brethren yet alive), that a greater harmony may subsist amongst us than at present apears from the behaviour of such as think themselves (tho' vainly) not
tyed down to good behaviour."

---

* Each Mason had his mark, and on some of the loose
sheets where the respective signatures are by the parties
themselves, their marks are appended.

1745   The "paucity of the Lodge" on the appointed day, however, prevented any business being taken up.

Our old friend, John Tulloch, had again been transgressing the rules of the Lodge. On the 30th of September he was "put to the award for entering aprentices in ye country of Petty without ye proper sanction of this Lodge, according to the regulations thereof. But in regaird the said John Tulloch was necessarly absent from this quarterly communication, the Tyler was ordered to acquaint him thereof, and yt. he answer the sd. complaint agt. the 15th Decr. next, with certification if he refuses yt. he will be expunged the Lodge as ane unworthy member thereof."

"Broyr. Rot. Nicolson put Lachlan Harrold and William M'Bain to the award, the first for being guilty of taking hewing stones from the complainer's property, and the latter for finishing a piece of work he was undertaken, both qch being heinous crimes, diametrically oposit to ye fundamental laws of Masonry, as well as ye pure prins. of a Free Masson, Br. Nicolson is ordered to bring in his proof of ye said facts agt. ye sd diet, or any day most convenient for both partys betwixt and yt. time." *

The '45.   The insurrection of 1745-46 dislocated the whole society of the Highlands, and its effects penetrated into our Mason Lodge. Some of its members had even taken up arms, of course on the side of the Government. The allusions, however, to the momen-

---

* On the 24th June 1745—"A letter was wrote to Captn. Scott anent his sergeants not attending the Lodge, the answer of which the Master is to communicate to the Brethren so soon as he receives the same."

tous events of this period are meagre and guarded; 1745 probably there were partisans of both sides members of the Lodge. On the 20th December 1745 it is recorded that the Lodge met " when very few of their number attended, on accot. of the present disturbance —several members being joyned to the independent companys." The independent companies here referred to, raised mainly through the loyalty and discretion of President Forbes of Culloden, were eighteen in number, and recruited among the clans who adhered to the Government. The 10th company was raised in the town of Inverness, and consisted of about 100 men under

William Mackintosh, Captain.
Kenneth Mathieson, Lieutenant.*
William Baillie, Ensign.

On the 27th of Decr. " upon account of the paucity of the Lodge," the meeting was dissolved and the business delayed; and the minute of 24th June 1746, bears that " the former communication upon Lady Day not being kept on account of the disorders of the times." And no wonder. On Lady Day 1746, the troops of Prince Charles Edward occupied Inverness, the independent companies, including that raised in the town, had retreated into Ross and Sutherland, and Cumberland was advancing to the field of Culloden, where the hopes of the Stuarts were finally dashed to pieces.

Chambers describes Inverness at this period to have been then only such a town as could be expected in the vicinity of a Highland half-civilised

* There were a Kenneth Mathison, Senr., and Kenneth Mathison, Junr., merchants in Inverness, entered apprentices 27th Decr. 1753.

territory—a Royal Burgh not yet emancipated from feudal dominion, a seaport, but possessing only a slight local commerce, confined in its dimensions, limited in population, and poor in resources. A coach at this time had never been seen in Inverness, nor was there a turnpike road within forty miles of its walls.

This is quoted from "Burt," and yet Burt says, in his fourth letter, written in 1725, "I was entertained with the surprise and amusement of the common people in this town, when, in the year 1725, a chariot with six monstrous great horses arrived here by way of the sea coast. An elephant exposed in one of the streets of London could not have excited greater admiration. One asked what the chariot was, another, who had seen the gentlemen alight, told the first, with a sneer at his ignorance, it was a great cart to carry people in, and such like. But since the making of some of the roads I have passed thro' them with a friend, and was greatly delighted to see the Highlanders run from their huts close to the chariot, and looking up, bow with their bonnets to the coachman, little regarding us that were within." This shows that roads were made fit for carriages in 1725 or shortly after.

The military roads were commenced in 1726, the first from Perth, *via* Glenalmond and Aberfeldy, to Dalnacardoch, the other *via* Dunkeld to Dalnacardoch, here they join and run on to Dalwhinnie, when they again diverge, one leading by Corryarrack to Fort-Augustus, the other by Ruthven and north to Inverness, and the next goes direct from Inverness, *via* Fort-Augustus, to Fort-William—these were all finished before 1740.

On the 25th March the mortcloth again appears The Mort-
in the minutes. The Master made a motion which
was unanimously agreed to, "that *a white border
should be put round the mortcloth*," and a committee
was appointed "to inspect the length and breadth of
the said cloth, and to report the same." At the
same meeting it was resolved, "for the more easy
payment of quarter pennies, that the samen should
be paid quarterly for the future," and threats of
"diligence" and expulsion from the Lodge of those
in arrears were minuted.

The price of provisions is incidentally referred to Price of
on the same date. The widow of William Mackay, meal.
mason in Nairn, having applied for relief from the
Lodge, on account "of the indigent state of her
familie, having sex childeren and nothing to support
them; they unanimously agreed to send her ten
shillings for to be delivered to Brother Sutherland,
at Nairn, to purchase one boll meall for her use."
From subsequent entries it appears that 10s. was
allowed to Widow Mackay as a yearly pension.

On the same day Brother Mackintosh of Cul-
chlachie reported that a great quantity of hewn
stones had been stolen from him. The operative
brethren were warned, upon pain of expulsion, not to
work for any person producing such stones, until
Brother Mackintosh was acquainted thereof, and was
satisfied, after inspection, that they were not his property.

On the 29th of September a petition was prepared for permission to erect a "loaft" in the
"Highland Kirk." The minute reads as follows :—

"The Master made a motion to the Lodge that

a second application should be made to the Session
for the priviledge of a building of a loaft in the
Highland Kirk, in terms of the former Act of Session
granted by them to us some years ago, which all
agreed to, and in order to facilitate the same in the
most peaceable manner, they ordain Donald Monro,
Junior Warden, and Donald M'Liss to waite jointly
on each of the ministers before the Session is applyed,
and they to return their answer to a committee to
meet at the Lodge the fifteenth day of November
next, or any other day betwixt this and that time
that shall be appointed."

On the 26th October 1750 the Master acquainted
the Lodge of his "having given in a memorial wt.
ane Act of Session in favours of the Lodge about 22
years agoe for their building a loft in ye Highland
Church, to ye Kirk Session, for their aprobation of
the same. But in regaird the Sacrament being to be
dispensed ye 4th Nov. next, they deferred af entering
into any publyc business until that was over. The
Mr. proposed that he and two oyr. members of the
Lodge should wait of the Session the first day they
met after ye Sacrament, and get a final ansr., qh.
was agreed to."

On the 30th November the Lodge met " to have returns of the Kirk-Session, when the report was made
that the Session was not pleased with the petition.
Therefore, they drew up another one, which, with the
Act of Session, was delivered to the Boxmaster, to
be by him and as many of the operative brethren as
now in town should wait on the Kirk-Session upon
the eleventh day of December next, to get a formal
answer as to that part."

The deliverance of the Kirk-Session, which quotes the petition of 1728, was given on 26th Febry. 1751 :—

" COPY OF DELIVERANCE.

"At Inverness, December 24th, 1728, in presence of Master Alexander Fraser, Moderator, Mr Daniel Mackenzie, Mr Alexander M'Bain, Assessors, and permanent members of the Kirk-Session there. The petition of the Masons of said burgh being again read, 'setting forth that they have no place in either of the churches of this Burgh for accommodating them to hear the word of God, by which means they are necessitate to stay at home, or walk in the fields on the Lord's Day in time of Divine worshipe, very much contrary to their inclinations, and seeing there is a vacancy in the east side of the new kirk, adjacent to that vacancy lately given to the wrights and coupers of this Burgh (wherein they have built a loaft), and that they are willing at their own ex- penses to erect a loaft for themselves in said vacancy, which will not, in their humble opinion, encroach upon any, and therefore craving that the Session would be pleased to grant them a tollerance and act in their favours to that effect.'

" Which petition being considered, and the Session having reasoned thereon, they did then remove to the said kirk, and having surveyed the space above specified, with respect to the common loaft in the south end of the said kirk, and also with respect to the seats below, and with respect to the lights of the said end of the kirk, and having thereafter returned

4

1751 to the Session-House and resumed consideration of
the said petition, found it reasonable to grant, as also
hereby do grant, the desire of the same. But for
preventing of any encroachments on the seats or
lights above named, the Session appoint the limits
and boundings of the said loaft to be as follows, viz.:
Primo, the said loaft may extend in length from the
face of the common loaft no nearer to the pulpit than
the distance of nine feet and an half. *Secundo*, the
lowest part of the breast of said loaft fronting the
pulpit, floaring and jests included, to be no further
downwards from the top of the hanging post on the
side wall of the kirk than ten foot three inches, and
the height of the breast from thence upwards to be
no more than three feet and three inches, viz., no
nearer to the top of the side post than seven foot.
Tertio, The breadth of the loaft from the side wall
towards the area of the kirk must advance no more
than seven feet and an half including the pillars, and
in case of any encroachment by these dimensions on
the sight or bearing of those who sit in the common
loaft as the seats of it are at present.

"The said Petitioners are (if neid be) at their own
charges to heighten the seats of the said common
loaft proportionally so as the sight and hearing of the
minister may be preserved to all that sit in that part
of the common loaft.

"And the Session did, and hereby do, grant to
the said Petitioners and their successors in trade, the
tollerance and permission sought in their said petition, with full power to them to build a loaft in the
space above and injoy the same in all time coming
providing always that they observe the dimensions

above narrated, and that they make the entry thereto 1751
thro' the middle of the breast of the said common
loaft. Whereupon act extracted forth of the records
of Session by me.

"ROBERT EDWARDS, C.F.G. Sess."

This Act was renewed by the Session on 24th February 1751, as appears by a docquet beneath the above.
And on the back of the parchment is the following:

"At Inverness, 26 Feby. 1751.
"The within Act, of date 24 Decr. 1728 and 26
Feby. 1751, was granted by the Session to the within
Masons, by the concurrance of Magistrates, Council,
and Heritors, with the Kirk Session of Inverness.
Extracude.

"ROBERT EDWARDS, C.F.G. Sess."

Having obtained the permission of the Session to
erect the long coveted loft in the church, the brethren
had to concert means for doing so; and on 25th
March they imposed a tax upon each member of one
penny sterling per week from the 9th of February
till Christmas day, "and that for enabling them to
build a loaft in the new Kirk of Inverness for themselves and families; and they ordain that the same
shall be punctually observed by clearing their payments thereof once a quarter; and to certify such
as shall be in arrear at the end of the last quarter,
that they shall have no priviledge to the said loaft
or seatt in the said church, until they pay £4 Scots
for the priviledge thereof."

On the 29th of June the members were earnestly
requested to pay up their pennies and arrears in

¹⁷⁵¹ order to enable the Boxmaster to purchase "the pillars and joists for their loft in the kirk, as well as to carry on the building thereof, as the same is immediately to be begun too : and the Boxmaster is ordered to use outmost diligence upon all bills in his custody without loss of time."

Another obstacle to the erection of their loft arises before the Brethren, and is thus recorded in their minutes of 30th September :—

"Then the Lodge, having considered the answer given to their petition to the Town Council anent their concurrance for building of our seats in the Highland Church, which was, that we should petition the Kirk Session (from whom we had an Act ratifyed in our favours for that effect), that they should relinquish any right they had in favours of the Town Councill and Heritors for erecting seatts in the Church, and then our petition should be heard.

"The Lodge, very well knowing that the Kirk Session always hade it in their power, and never were comptrolled before in granting such libertys, they therefore unanimously agree to petition the Heritors for their concurrence with the Session, and thereafter to be determined with the advice of that reverend body how to proceed; and they order the said memoriall to be drawn up, and carried by three brethren, viz., Alexr. Fraser, Donald M'Liss, and John Dunbar, to the severall Heritors, and to report the same upon their petition, when the Lodge is to be appointed *pro re nata* to determine what is to be done."

There is no further mention of the loft in the

Church for three and a half years, but it appears as 1755
if, in the interval, the Lodge had obtained full permission to proceed with its erection. At any rate,
they had purchased materials for this purpose. A
minute of the 25th March 1755 bears :—

" At same time (*i.e.*, in a meeting of committee
upon 16th January), there was a motion made anent
the ruinous condition of the timber bought for the
seat, and the improbability of obtaining the end for
which it was purchased. It was therefore directed
that Donald Fraser, Alexr. Grant, John Munro, and
Alexander Fraser, with first convenience, should view
and inspect the same where it lyes, so as it might be
somehow disposed of to the best advantage, as the
Lodge should think expedient and direct at their
first quarterly communication."

On the 1st December 1755, it was resolved :—

"That the haill timber lying in the Kirk, and proposed formerly for a seat, should be sold off to the
best advantage, upon Saturday, the sixth current, at
twelve o'clock, and payable by the purchaser or pur-
chasers at the term of Whitsunday next, on their
finding good security."

A note added to the above minute records that
"according to appointment, the timber was roupt at
£7. 18s. 3d. stg., and payment and security therefore
was granted to the Boxmaster therefor."

On the 25th March 1756, "the Boxmaster, being
asked if or not he had got the bills for wood mentioned in former minutes accepted, and in his hands,

¹⁷⁵⁶ and he answering he had not, he is hereby appointed to get the bills accepted, and lodge the same in the box again the next meeting."

The "irrepressible" John Tulloch has again got into trouble! This time his offence is against the Six Incorporated Trades, and is thus recorded in the minutes of 29th September.—

"The Convener of the Six Incorporated Trades gave in a petition agd. John Tulloch, for infringing the priviledges of the Wrights Incorporation, by working within their bounds, which being made appear to the Lodge as fact, they unanimously agreed to censure him for the said crime, and discharging him for the future to work at any calling that may in the least hurt any of the Six Incorporated Trades, under no less penalty than being expunged this Lodge as ane unworthie member thereof in order to maintain good harmonie."

On the 25th March following John was again put to the award. His crime on this occasion was having "received, entered, and admitted four apprentices without the advice and consent of the Master and Wardens. John's friends were of good standing,

> James McPherson in Calder,
> Donald McPherson, brother to Cluney,
> McIntosh of Corribrough, and
> His brother-in-law, one McKerquhar.

He was severely censured for this irregular proceeding, and ordered to pay to the Treasurer the dues of their entry; but John's reply was characteristic— "that for the two former he can give no other account of the fees due the Lodge than *that he drunk it.*" He was ordered to pay the dues, 26s., to the Treasurer by the 1st of June; but from the minutes of the 24th of that month it appears the same had not been paid, as he is again enjoined, upon pain of expulsion, to pay the above sum, with five shillings of penalty. Poor John, however, seems about this period to have had sentence of expulsion from this world and all its troubles, as well as from St John's Lodge, for there is no further allusion to him in the minutes; and from his previous character, it is more than probable he would have been a cause of some trouble to the Lodge had he been in life. Gone himself, however, he left a legacy to them which, as we shall afterwards see, was onerous and troublesome— viz., the guardianship of his son Donald, and the management of some houses for behoof of the widow and son.

The Masons resolved on 29th September to be incorporated with the other trades of Inverness.

"The Master made a motion to the Lodge that application should be made for their being incorporated with the other trades of this towne, which was agreed to, and a memoriall ordered to be drawn up by the Master, to be laid before the Grand Lodge for their interest in promoving the same, and the samen is ordered to be ready againe the thirteenth day of November nixt."

On the 28th December, five members who had absented themselves from the meeting that day, were

1757 expunged the Lodge "until they shall make a solemn recantation of their error, and then be by the Brethren received."

On the 9th of March following, two members were "erased out of the list of members of this Lodge, as having contemptuously disobeyed the order of the said Lodge, denying their presence at all occasions for some years past, tho' frequently advised thereto;" and three others were required to give in final answers by next meeting "why they did not attend for last year."

On the 15th December it was enacted "that the man having office in the Lodge that shall be absent on any account whatsomever," shall be fined 2s. 6d.; and in case any of the Boxmasters shall be absent, they shall not only pay the fine, but be obliged to pay for a new book, or any other damage the box may have sustained through being opened, "if it was to the value of the said box."

The processions and attendance at church were regular features of St John's Day, and on the 15th December, "It was unanimously agreed to make our procession from Brother M'Bean's house to the church upon St John's Day, being a preaching day, and from thence to the Lodge, without musick." On the 24th December, "The Lodge appointed the Box-masters to meet at the Lodge by nine o'clock St John's Day morning, and take out the proper jewells, and with the polls and robes to be carried to Brother M'Bean's house, from whence the Lodge is to proceed by 10 o'clock in the forenoon to church to hear Bror. M'Bean preach, and from thence to the Lodge to solemnize the day; and that a list of the whole members of the Lodge be given this evening to the

Tyler, with a certificate on the end yrof acquaint- Processions
ing all Brethren that none will be admitted to the
Lodge after ye procession, except such as attended
the same to church." The Minute of 27th December
records that a full Lodge met in the ordinary hall
at Brother Grant's, after the procession to and from
the church.

Notice of the funeral of George Cuthbert of
Castlehill, and of the fact of the "mortcloth" having
been used at it, occurs in the minutes of 24th Dec.
"George Nicholson made a demand upon the Lodge
for attending the founderall of our late Right Worshipful Master, George Cuthbert of Castlehill, for
one shilling for carring the mortcloth to Castlehill
at his interment, in absence of the proper Tyler, as
he alleged he lost a day's work thereby, for which the
present Master [Archibald Graham] paid one shilling
out of his own pocket." From this entry it appears
it was the duty of the Tyler to carry the mortcloth
to the funeral of members.

24th Decr. 1748.—" It was moved and agreed to Pensions
that a yearly pention should be allowed to indigent
persons belonging to the Lodge or such of their
relations as may call for charity." It was the
laudable custom of the Lodge to take into consideration the cases of poverty arising among the Brethren
or amongst their relatives, and, generally on St
John's Day, small donations were allotted to each at
the discretion of the Lodge. In St Andrew's Lodge
the same practice was observed, but this was apparently liable to abuse, and the Brethren were
cautioned against adopting all petitions coming before them from "other people, as our funds are
little enough to support our own poor." On the

1748 27th December the cases of Alexander Harrold and
Helen Nicolson were considered, and pensions of
10s. yearly were allowed to them, to be paid quarterly
if they wished it.   At the same meeting, John
M'Cool Taylor, "a poor old decayed tradesman,"
was granted two shillings, and Roderick M'Leod.three
shillings *and three pence halfpenny.*

The old feeling against those absenting themselves
from the meetings of the Lodge appears again in the
minutes of 10th January, specially directed against
those who thought themselves superior to the rest
of the Brethren.   "It was ordained that a list of
members be taken out on the end of this Book that
are thought worthy for regard that several of the
Brethren despize their meeting with us, not only
upon quarterly communications, but even upon St
John's Day when legaly called and charged theretoo.
Whereby the honor of Masonry is not only despised
by them, but an unnecessary charge left upon the
few that countenance the same."   Thereafter it was
resolved "that such members as are absent this day
shall be struck out of the list of the Lodge.   That
our harmony may be the better, as such Brethren
have been several times admonished of this our intention, which they seem altogether to despize and
neglect—allowing always such Brethren as were absent last St John's Day and now present at this
meeting to be inrowled on paying half-a-crown each
to the poor box, as an equivalent to the expence of
each member of that day, which they may, with
other absent members, are in ten days to pay to the
Boxmaster, if they incline to be continued members
of this Lodge, which if they fail to do after being advised thereof, they will for ever stand discharged as

Brethren of this Lodge and deprived of all immuni- 1749
ties thereof."

On the 15th December another shot is fired at
the absentees. The Master is ordained to certify to
the absent Brethren " that those that does not attend
next St John's Day's procession shall be excluded
the Lodge, as not only do they not attend on that
day, but other quarterly days as well."

The number of absentees on St John's Day was
no less than eleven, and among them were John
Mackintosh of Culchlachy, Duncan Fraser, Gillies
Kerr, William Robertson of Inshes, &c. The Lodge
were very indignant at their conduct. Not only
were they absent "in contempt of the former sede-
runts," but they had " declared their intention soe
to doe except when they pleased themselves." They
were granted " ane indulgence " to the 10th of
January to attend the Lodge, and then " to beg
pardon for their transgression "—otherwise they were
to be expunged. On the 10th, four of the offenders
appeared, and stated " that all their intention in
shifting the procession on St John's Day was on account that they did not apprehend it consisted with
MASONRY." This answer seems to have nonplussed
the Lodge for the time, as they adjourned till the
30th, when the same Brethren compeared, and the
Master, after a short lecture on the relevancy of a
procession as consistent with MASONRY, again granted
an indulgence to " the haill Brethren not conform-
ing," as well absent as present, to give in answers
against the 15th of March.

On the 26th March, John Monro, Gillies Kerr,
and Donald Fraser appeared, and stated that they
would not walk in procession on St John's Day.

1750   The Lodge unanimously agreed that they and all Brethren "whatsomever" absenting themselves on any quarterly communication, and "especially on the grand festival procession," shall not be admitted as a member of the Lodge after St John Baptist's Day next ensuing.

On the 14th December all the Brethren were ordered to attend the procession on St John's Day, "by ten o'clock that forenoon, at Brother M'Bean's house in Castle Street;" those that did not attend were not to be admitted as Brethren in future.

On the 27th December, St John's Day, the orthodox Brethren accordingly met at Brother M'Bean's house, and after making the usual procession, the Lodge was opened, when "five of the seceding brethren demanded admittance, which was refused them until they acknowledged: To make a solemn recantation of their error, which was sent them by way of a friendly memoriall and advyse to return to their dutie, and required their answer on the foot thereof: But, instead of giving the Lodge that satisfaction, they carried the memoriall off, and sent a very scurrilous answer, without touching one point thereof. Therefore, they are again, for the last time, advised to give their promise to answer against the eleventh of January next: Otherwise, they shall stand expunged the Lodge for ever."

On the 2d February 1751, another last appeal was to be made to the offending Brethren :—"The Master proposed treating with the Brethren that deny the charge of the Lodge, in order to bring them back to obedience before the same be laid before the Grand Lodge, which the Lodge agreed to."

From the absence of any allusions to absentees

for a very long period afterwards, it may be pre- 1761 sumed that the strong measures here indicated had proved effective. It was not till the 27th of December 1761 that reference is made to such offenders, when we read:—

"The meeting observing and considering with regrate that the members doe not attend there quarterly meetings, they, therefore, unanimously resolve and enact, That each absent member, especially on St John's Day, shall pay one shilling sterling for and toward payment of the dener (dinner) alwise prepared of that day for the Brethren, certifying such as shall either wilfully absent or refuse to pay, that they shall be discharged the Lodge priviledges and immunities thereof."

On the 27th December 1763 "it was unanimously agreed and resolved upon, that every member absenting, and who do not pay their dues regularly, shall be scored out of our lists and record, and extruded the Lodge privileges and immunities thereof, and a regular roll of the continued and deserving members is of this date commenced accordingly."

"December 27.—A meeting appointed to hold on the first Tuesday of every month, beginning with the first Tuesday of February next, "upon which day it is hoped the Brethren will attend, pay any bygone arrears, and such as does not attend will be scored of the list, and have no privileges of thus Lodge."

The case of Alexander Fraser occupied the Lodge for some time. The first entry against him occurs on 10th January, when we read :—

1764   " Alexander Fraser being not only drunk, but
gave very grate offence to the Lodge by oprobious
language, and after being twice ordered out, contrair
to the good rules and decent decorum of the Lodge,
brock open the door thereof, and entered the same in
a very rude and unmannerly way, for which he was
fined in five shillings sterling, to be put into the
poor's box, and every member discharged to lift a tool
in his service until he pay the said five shillings, and
crave pardon of the Lodge for offence."

On the 25th March, "Alexander Fraser being
absent, the former sederunt was read. The whole
Lodge unanimously confirmed the former decree, in
his paying five shillings ster. to the poor's box, and
making a proper acknowledgment to the Lodge for
the offence given at their last meeting, and they
ordained the Tyler to intimate this to him." The
minute informs us, probably to mark the contrast
with Alexander's uproarious behaviour, that "the
Lodge was orderly and *douccley* shut," and adjourned
till the 24th of June, "extraordinary occasions excepted."

On the 1st of May, "the minute of the 10th
Jany. last, relating to Alexr. Fraser's behaviour,
confirmed by the Lodge of 25th March last, was
read in presence of the said Alexr. Fraser, and his
answers demanded, whether he inclined to comply
with the sentence of the Lodge or not. To which
he submitted, by begging pardon in common form,
and the Lodge a third time affirmed the decree on
paying five shillings sterling into the poor's box, for
which he granted a bill payable on demand."

This pretty severe fine on an operative mason,

and the ample apology required from him, seems to
have been necessary at the period, but I am glad to
say that the mere possibility of such cases arising at
the present day is very remote.

We have before seen that the Masons had an The Trades House.
interest in the Trades House, and by their minute of
24th June—

"The Lodge agreed that the Six Incorporate
Trades should be brought to accompt for their intromissions for the rent of the Trades House since
Whitsunday Javij and fourty-five, and that the
Master should call a Generall Meeting of the sd.
Trades for that effect betwixt and the latter end
of July next, when the Whitsunday rents are all
cleared; and they ordain, That an overture be made
in the General Meeting of the Trades, That an yearly
accompt. thereafter be stated by the Genl. Boxmaster, That each trade may have their yearly pro-
portion of the sd. Rents for the future."

On the 29th Sept. it is reported that the Master
had not yet been able to settle with the Trades, and
the above order is continued. On the 30th Nov. the
account was made up, when it was found there was
a balance due to the Masons on the four years rents
of £4. 17s. 3d. As the Masons share seems to have
been one-seventh, this would make the yearly rent
equal to £8. 2s. 6d.

Some years later, on 12th Nov. 1753, there was
an adjustment of accounts between the Six Incorporate Trades and the Mason Lodge relating to "the
Trades, &c., Mason's House." A docquet, attached
by the Trades to the accounts, declares "that they

would maintain the handbell to the Masons as they did for themselves." It is probable that this refers to the hand-bell rung at funerals, a custom which, perhaps, some Brethren may remember to have lingered till a late period in Inverness. The practice of preceding a funeral by a party ringing a hand-bell was common in most towns. In Kirkwall the following rhyme was said to have been repeated by the functionary, who was clothed in a long robe or gown, with wide sleeves:—

> " Come to your long home,
>   Built of lime and clay and stone."

On the 1st December 1755 Donald Fraser represented to the Lodge that there is "£4 str. p. bill drawn by him on Castlehill" still due, " by serving the Incorporated Trades and Masons for the Trades House," and he states that the Trades were willing to pay six parts of said bill. The Lodge, upon that condition, " and out of regard he is a brother," agreed to pay their seventh part.

A committee was appointed to meet at the Saracen's Head 'twixt four and five of the evening of the 15th December " to wait on the Trades to count with them, the Trades, about the Lodge's share of the profits or rents arising from the houses in common with the Lodge and the Six Incorporated Trades."

The committee accordingly " having met with the Six Incorporated Trades, when, at stating of the accompts, the sum of £2. 16s. 7d. stg. fell to the Masons as their share, besides a seventh part of the sum of £9 as the rent payable by Mr M'Bean, minister, due at Whitsunday last."

One shilling was "paid for as *incidents* with the 1755 Trades."

On the 26th of January 1762 the Lodge had a 1762 compt and reckoning with the Trades "for the rents arising to the Lodge from their house since the last clearance."

"The Deacon-Conveener of the Trades produced a state of their intromissions and receivings for and from Whity. 1758 to Whity. 1761, including a year's rent of Mr M'Bean's lodgeing formerly outstanding, amounting to £69 stg." The repairs for those years were £15. 10s., and the balance £53. 10s., whereof fell to the Lodge £7. 12s. 10d. The Lodge discharge the Trades of "all proceedings . . . . with this exception that they are lyable and to accompt for a share of what shall be recovered or made from the old windows of the house," &c. In witness whereof, &c., the minute is signed by the Deacon-Convener of the Trades and the Master of the Lodge.

Several other entries occur in the minutes respecting the Trades House, but they are generally of the same nature as those already quoted, and need not be repeated.

On the 2d *May* 1780 the Lodge finally dispose of their seventh share in the Trades House, and the record of the transaction follows:—

"Brother William Cuming reported to the meeting that in consequence of the unanimous approbation and desire of the Lodge, the seventh share of the Old Trades House, the property of this Lodge, was sold and disposed to the Six Incorporated Trades of Inverness at their last General Meeting, for the sum of —— sterling.

"The Lodge unanimously approve of the above bargain, and empower the Master and officers to grant an ample conveyance of the said seventh share to the Six Incorporated Trades with all convenient speed, and appoint the sum arising from the foresaid sale to be applied for carrying on the new Lodge."

On the 30th of January, "Donald M'Eandry, Irish precentor, was ordered five shillings ster. to be paid by the Boxmaster," and again a like sum on 26th March.

Dec. 27.—James Wilson, an itinerant brother from Banff, admitted on paying £8 Scots for the mortcloath.

The support of the mortcloth appears to have caused the Brethren some anxiety. On the 2d of February a motion was agreed to, "that for the support of our mortcloath the same should be lett out to people burying in the neighbouring parishes."

The Boxmaster, Thomas Tulloch, seems to have been unfortunate in his book-keeping, for when his accounts were required on the 30th November, they were "not ready," and being produced on the 18th Decr., they are found to be "confused and irregular, and so, in that situation, cannot be settled." Therefore he was ordered to prepare them "in a formal way," in order to be settled again St John's Day. Accordingly, on the 27th December his accounts are read and passed, in a minute filling nearly the whole of a closely-written page, too long to be here quoted, when the balance found due by him was *sixteen shillings and sevenpence halfpenny sterling*, which account is boldly engrossed in large half-text.

At the meeting on 18th December the Brethren

resolved to change their Lodge to the house of
Alexander Clark, vintner' in the Castle Wynd. At
the same meeting they gave up one of the contested
points with "the seceding Brethren," and declare
that "a procession of the Lodge is looked upon as
idle, and on that account dispensed with."

On the 25th March 1752, the Lodge having
taken into consideration "the low and distressed
circumstances of Christian Ker, relict of the decease
John Dick, and three infant children," grant her a
yearly pension of 20s. sterling.

Fort-George was at this period in course of
erection, and there naturally the operative members
of the craft in the North would be found. There
were no quarterly meetings held from 25th March to
1st November, when the Master represented that he
had not convened these meetings as "all or most of
the Operative Brethren were either working in the
country or employed in the public works at the Point
of Ardersier, and for that reason he thought it unnecessary to convene the few Geometrical Brethren
who live in the Burgh, and more particularly that
he thought it a hardship that any of them should
be called from their work at any time of the last
straitning season, which called aloud for their utmost
diligence. And now the Master hopes that the
members now present will approve of these his
reasons for not inditing a Meeting in each of the
months of June and September last, according to the
forms of the Lodge, and which they all now do,
returning him their thanks for the laudable reason
he assigns."

The conclusion of this minute is quaint: "Thereafter the meeting proceeded to other points of busi-

1752

Fort-George

1752 ness, but as the night is far advanced they suspend
minuting the same until next meeting."

The Master again omits to call the Brethren together upon St Andrew's Day. His excuse is not
so happy as the last, but from the jovial proposal
with which he wound up his speech, it was well
received by the Brethren. On the 18th December :—

" The Master represented to the meeting that he
would have conveened a meeting of the Lodge upon
the 30th day of Nov. last, but that he was upon that
day in the country upon business he could not absent
himself from, and acknowledges himself faulty in not
giving notice of his absence, that the members then
in town might celebrate that day, being St Andrew's,
so remarkably observed by Masons. And *now* that
we have the pleasure to meet again, and *that* we are
informed George Drummond, Esquire, Lord Provost
of Edinburgh, was elected upon that day Grand
Master of Scotland, the Master proposes to drink
to his health, and to those who composed his meeting
at the Grand Election, with three (probably three
cheers), which the meeting of this Lodge unanimously
approved of and agreed to, and at the same time excused the Master for his absence, as it was necessary.

"*Thereafter*" the question was debated whether
St John's Day next should be held according to the
new or old style, when the Lodge candidly records
that they " find a difficulty in answering the motion."
At any rate, "rather than blunder," they postpone
their decision, and appoint a committee to meet upon
the 21st and decide for them. The committee having
met, resolve that in future their meetings shall be
held according to the New Style.

On the 27th December 1752, Duncan Forbes, 1752
merchant, has his admission recorded in the following terms :—

"Duncan Forbes, merchant in Inverness, represented that from the regaird he has to Masonry, and
the members of this Honble. Lodge, he proposes to
the meeting to associate himself with them henceforth, and to pay quarter pennys, if it will be agreeable to the Lodge. The proposal being accordingly
stated, the Lodge unanimously agreed he should be
a member with them, and appoints the Boxmaster to
add him to the roll, and to charge him with quarter
pennies from this date. And the said Duncan Forbes hereby dispenses with any right he might pretend to the mortcloth of the Lodge, and declares his
association with them cannot be construed a right
thereto."

This part of the minute is thereupon signed
"Duncan Forbes" in a bold old-fashioned hand—
older than that of the period.

On the 12th December the Lodge resolve to
walk in procession if their sister lodge did so likewise, "but if they resolve against it, then the procession of this Lodge will be suspended in regard of
the paucity of our numbers." The minutes of 27th
December make no mention of a procession, and it is
apparent none was made.

"January 11.—The Reverend Mr John Grant,
minr. of the Gospel, at Dores, and William Mack
Leod, merchant, in Sky, were this night entred as
apprentices to the Lodge, and a short lecture by way

1753 of instruction given them upon the entrd. prentice part of Masonry, when the latter promised to satisfy Brother Geddes this night for the fees of his entry, and that of the former complimented to him because of his calling as a minister of the Gospel, who as such will give spiritual advice to the Lodge, and may be instrumental in promoting that harmony and love which should subsist among Masons, and our Reverend Brother Grant gave his mite to the poor's box, and thanked the Lodge for the honour done him."

The Rev. John Grant here mentioned was Missionary at Fort-Augustus, called to the parish of Dores in March, and admitted 1st May 1753.

There were five entered apprentices made at the meeting of 13th February: three were entered for ten shillings each, and two at five shillings each, " besides an entertainment to the members."

On the 25th March, the Boxmaster being questioned about his accounts, answered "that hitherto he could not make them out regularly, in regard that the account of quarter pennies he received last John's Day had dropt from him, or rather suspected it might have been in the box." On examination it *was* found there.

On the same day it is recorded that " as the Incorporated Trades have very laudably made a contribution for the Rev. Mr Paul, assisting pastor in this place, so it was proposed to the meeting what they would order to be paid him on that account; and the question being stated what the same should be, it was unanimously agreed that one pound one shilling sterling be paid to those collecting for this Revd.

Pastor's behoof. And for the payment of this sum 175s
the meeting appointed Kenneth Mathieson, senr.,
and Thomas Clark, merchants, to pay each of them
10s., being the dues of their entries as apprentices to
this Lodge, and they accordingly agree to do the
same; and Mr Mathieson is appointed as one of the
collectors of this contribution for Mr Paul, to mark
the Masons as advancers of this sum, which, with one
shilling sterling now advanced to him by the boxmaster, completes the Masons' compliment; and the
saids Kenneth Mathieson and Thomas Clark are
hereby severally discharged of their dues to the box
as entered apprentices, and the Master recommends
to the haill Brethren to give what further compliment
they incline from their private purses."

An objection appears to have been taken to the
entry of an apprentice to Mr Adams, architect at
Fort-George. The minutes of 30th November record
that the Master had, in a full Lodge of Masons
on the previous day, entered Rodrick Mackenzie,
apprentice to Mr Adams, architect at Fort-George,
as an entered apprentice, and that he had paid the
dues of his admission; "but in regard some of the
members of this meeting had started some objections
to the entry, the Master and meeting supersede entitling him to the privileges of the Lodge until St
John's Day next, that the character of the sd. Robert
M'Kenzie may be ascertained, and the objections
started removed."

On the 27th December accordingly, " the objections with regard to the entry of Rodrick M'Kenzie
as a member of this Lodge spoke to by a member
yrof and answers made thereto by others, and ye
whole heard and considered off by the Lodge, they

1753 by a great majority of votes found him, the said
Rodrick M'Kenzie, an improper person to be entitled
to any of the benefits of the Lodge, and reject him
as such, and ordain the Boxmaster to repeate and
pay to the said Rodrick M'Kenzie any sums paid
by him," &c.

On the 15th December the Lodge resolved that
their future meetings should be held in Brother
James Geddes's house, and removed from Widow
Clark's.

From the year 1751 downwards we find that the
Lodge, through their Boxmaster, intromitted with the
rents of some houses which belonged to John Tulloch
for the behoof of his widow and children. Whether
this was our old offending friend John does not appear, but his last entry as a culprit was in 1748.
There is a loose copy of an "Accompt Debr. and
Credr." betwixt the Lodge and their Boxmaster on
account of the deceased *Donald* Tulloch, mason, his
houses," for the year 1752-1753. In the minutes,
and even in the docquet to the same account, it is invariably styled *John* Tulloch's concern. This account
exhibits some curious entries. There were altogether
seven tenants, paying a total rental of only £5. 7s. 8d.
The following are some of the entries :—

	s.	d.
To 2 thraw drawing straw, at 10d.		
pr. thraw - - - -	1	8
To 500 scobs, at 2½d. per 100 -	1	2
To a band to Margaret Munro's		
door of the house - - -	0	6
To a rail to Hugh M'Bean's house -	0	4
To a thatcher - - - -	0	6
To pease given Widow Tulloch -	1	5

August 1753—	S.	D.	1753
To Widow Tulloch, ½ boll bear -	6	0	
To the schoolmaster for the boy -	3	6	
To a pair shoes to the boy - -	1	4	
To 3 thraw drawing straw, at 10d.			
p. thraw - - - -	2	6	
To 3 thraw do., at 9d. per thraw -	2	3	
To 900 scobs, at 2½d. per 100 -	1	10½	
To the thatcher - - - -	1	8	
To a load divotts - - - -	0	2	
To incident charges with the tenents			
and oyrs. on this affair - -	4	6	

The minutes of the 25th March 1755 record that on the 16th January, in a committee of the Lodge, "there was a motion that a meeting should forthwith ensue with the relict and children of John Tulloch, to settle anent the intromissions of the Lodge with the defunct's tenements, at sight of any number of their friends, and John Munro, Alexander Fraser, Donald M'Liss, Gillies Kerr, John Dunbar, and the Boxmaster, together with the Master and Secretary, was appointed to meet thereanent accordingly upon the fifth day of March then next now current."

No less than eight persons appointed as parties on one side to settle accounts amounting to £5. 7s. 8d. per annum! We are fond of repeating to-day that "time is money." At that period it must have been at a heavy discount!

The committee met accordingly, when "the defunct's widow and son, and Hugh Tulloch, tenant in Calder, their friend and confident, present. There was a fitted accompt in the way of charge and discharge made up, and the ballance arising therefrom

1755 in favours of the Lodge, was properly and regularly ascertained and approven of by the parties, conform to the accompt."

"Thereafter Donald Tulloch, John's son, preferred a petition setting forth his desire of continueing at school to learn book-keeping. And the meeting was inclined to think such branch of education could not fully tend to get him a livelihood, he then being of age fit for a trade, wherefore it was recommended to him 'twixt and this day to consider and determine what business or trade he would incline to follow, and then to attend and produce his books to be laid before the meeting."

On the 27th December 1756 the Boxmaster was directed to have his accounts made up and laid before a committee of the Lodge, upon the 25th of January, when "John Tulloch's widow and son are appointed to attend to see the accompts adjusted as to the intromissions wh. the rents of the said deceast John Tulloch."

There is a curious transaction about some books purchased for the Lodge by one of the Brethren. On the 25th March we read—

"Brother Kerr having, by order and direction of the Lodge, commissioned for three books containing the rules and regulations to be observed, and the songs to be sung in the Lodge, and the expense thereof, including postages, amounting to £3. 10s., the Boxmaster is appointed to repay Brother Kerr of his advances for the books."

"Mr Kerr was paid . . . £1. 10s. 10d. in full

of the price of the books taken from Mr Kerr, and 1757
therefore he discharged the Lodge; and thereafter,
upon a motion made of giving the books back to
himself at a discount, he accordingly took them back
again, and granted bill for the same, being £2 sterling, payable Martinmas next."

Dec. 23.—William Mackay, apprentice to Andrew
Smith, mason in Kinloss, and lawful son to the deceast William Mackay, mason in Nairn, was entered
as an apprentice " gratis, on account that some of
the Brethren present represented his deceast father
as a worthy member of this Lodge."

Dec. 27.—" A subscription paper was produced
and subscribed by a number of the Brethren, and
which subscription paper was recommended by the
Master to Brethren to be encouraged as tending to
the good and wellfare of the Society."

Scattered throughout the minutes are several
notices of the admission of apprentices by two or
three members met at various times and places. On
the 30th November 1757, Robert Edwards, Senior
Warden, and a quorum of the Brethren, report that
on the 21st they had admitted and received Robert
Anderson, silversmith, a member of the Lodge. This
was approven of, but " thereafter it was unanimously
agreed to and enacted, that henceforward no select
number shall upon any pretext whatever take upon
themselves to enter apprentices, &c., without the
advice and consent of the Master . . . and other
officers, and a just and perfect Lodge with them convened, upon the pain of forfeiting for each offence,
not only a sum adequate to the ordinary dues payed

1757 by intrants, but also in the further sum of five
shillings sterling money, for the use of the poor of
the Lodge."

At the same meeting they adjourned till St
John's Day "at or before 10 o'clock of the forenoon
of that day," when the Brethren were recommended
" to attend chapterly accordingly."

On the 27th December, after the election of
office-bearers, " the Master appointed the Boxmaster
to " pay the Tylor his shoes in the usuall way."

On the same day " it was moved to the meeting
that Brother Fraser should have some certain annuall
allowance for his care of, and keeping, the mortcloath intire and tight, and it was unanimously agreed
that he should be free of quarter pennies, and two
shillings sterling over and above."

1758   On the 30th of November 1758, "the Lodge
having taken it into their serious consideration that,
since their last meeting Gillies Kerr, Senior Warden,
has deceased and indebted to the Lodge by bill £2
sterling, and as he was by all the Brethren greatly
esteemed, and leaving a wife and child not in an
opulent way, by unanimous consent, they order the
bill to be cancelled."

Thereafter there was a motion made by the
Master, " That Robert Edwards, a Member of this
Lodge, has for some time past been guilty of diverse
irregularities unbecoming a Mason, and too numerous
to be here enumerated : Therefore, and that Brother
Edwards may have a free and impartial tryal for
these irregularities," a committee was appointed " to
draw up Articles of Impeachment agt. the said
Brother Edwards of the particular of these irregularities, and these articles being drawn up, to intimat

the same to Brother Edwards, and he is to sist himself personally before a committee appointed by the Master upon the 5th day of December next, with power to the committee to take the Articles of Impeachment into their consideration with the evidence then offered, and report the same to the whole Lodge upon St John's Day next, on which day the said Brother Edwards is also to attend, with certification that if Brother Edwards doe not attend the committee upon said day they will report the same to the Lodge, and proceed to jugement thereon as if Brother Edwards had confessed the whole articles."

The returns to the Grand Lodge appear to have been rendered with considerable irregularity by most of the Lodges throughout the country. An advertisement was inserted "in the public papers" by the Grand Lodge, appointing that a return should be made immediately after St John's Day of the Master and Wardens of each Lodge, to Mr Alexr. Macdougal, Grand Secretary. Our Lodge appointed Mr Hugh Monro, secretary, to make such return, and to correspond with Mr Macdougal.

The "quarter pennies" seem to have been in a 1760 chronic state of arrear. There are continual references to this occurring in the minutes, and the verbal denunciations and "earnest appeals" to the members are frequent, but apparently of no great effect. We have seen that a number of years previously the Lodge took very strong steps for their collection, and on the 24th January 1760 they indicate that they must again resort to legal steps. The minute bears—"A list of arrears due to the Lodge was made up, which the Master took charge of, to talk in the first instance to the respective debitors,

1760 resolving that if they do not comply and pay, the
same will be put in the hands of a person of business,
that they may be prosecute as accords."

On the 29th September following a "list and
state of the bills and outstandings by accompt,
which by appointment was given out with the
vouchers so far to Brother Duncan Grant, writer, to
whom it was earnestly recommended to recover payment from all concerned, in regard they have in
view to accummulate and give the whole on proper
security."

1768   On the 20th December 1768 it is intimated that
"any Brethren in debt to the Thesaurer are to pay
the same 'twixt and St John's Day, when there is
to be a new roll made up, and none in arrears is to
be admitted in this Lodge.

Dec. 1.—The Lodge having settled down for
business, or as it is expressed in the minutes, "being
inclined so to do, and preparing for that 'end,'"
were interrupted by "some Members of the sister
Lodge, . . . which made the going on with the
intended business not so proper at this dyet," and it
was accordingly adjourned till next meeting.

On the 8th December the Master proposed that
the next meeting should be held on the 22d, and that
it may "be as throng as possible, when he proposed
that *every* Brother shall be prepared to speak for
their mutuall edification." Accordingly, on the 22d
December it is recorded that "the Brethren inclosed
lectured each of them on Masonry agreeable to their
severall capacitys and abilitys."

From a transaction recorded under date 27th
January 1762, we learn that five per cent. was the
interest charged on a loan for twelve months. The

Lodge having called up their arrears, advanced £22 1767 to Doctor Alex. Monro and John Monro, couper, upon their joynt bill, payable a year after date, for £23. 2s., or at about the rate of 4¾ per cent. discount. The bill seems to have run on with accruing interest for about five years. On the 10th January 1767 we read :—

" There was a clearance with John Munro, couper, anent his bill, conjunct with Doctor Monro, which, with interest, amounts the 27th current to £26. 11s. sterling. John Munro payed £13. 11s., and the balance due is £13, of which there was a discharged account, and the same marked on the back of the bill, the money lodged in the box."

June 2.—Mr John Fraser, minister, admitted to the Lodge this day. He "was exeemed from the dues by the Lodge."

The office-bearers elected on 27th December 1764 1764 were—

Captain John Gregor, Master.
John Fraser and Simon Fraser, Wardens.
Duncan Forbes, Secretary.
William Sharp and John Macpherson, Stewards.

This election is worthy of being noted as one of importance. From a letter dated in 1770, a copy of which I found on a loose sheet of paper (afterwards given in extenso), it is bailed as a new era in the history of the Lodge when the operative Brethren were ousted from its management, on account of their indolence, &c. It explains also an improved public

1764   spirit and discipline in the Lodge, which may be re-marked from this period, particularly in the scheme for the erection of a permanent building for their Lodge, and the renewal of the annual processions on St John's Day. While, however, the records of the Lodge henceforth appear to be more regularly and accurately kept, they lose a good deal of that quaintness and *naïveté* which have previously amused us.

Feb. 5—" The Master represented that, in order to regulate the affairs of the Lodge, improve the Brethren, and bring them forward in the knowledge and spirit of Masonry, a meeting shall happen and hold of the Brethren the first Tuesday of each month."

On the same day it was moved, "That Wm. Alexander, dancing master, sometime agoe promitted a member of this Lodge, had lately misbehaved, and therefore should be extruded this Lodge, and expunged from our books and Society." This was unanimously agreed upon, and the same intimated to him.

The earlier practice of the Lodge had apparently been to allow the arrears of quarter pennies and other dues to lie in the hands of each member who granted a bill for the amount. This custom had lately been done away with, and the more regular one adopted of calling up the arrears and placing the sums out at interest. Seeing the favourable result of this alteration in the management of their balance, the Lodge, after several meetings " examining into the state of our funds, and makeing such scheme and view thereof as will clear up and make same equal and easie hereafter," feel emboldened to take higher views, and on the 2d April 1765 we have the first hint of that admirable project which subsequently culminated in the erection of the extensive building which is now **1765** our property.

"The Master [Captain John Gregor], Brother Cumming, Brother Munro, and Brother Grant, are appointed to draw up a form of a circulating letter to be laid before this Lodge, in order for their approbation, that the same may be transmitted to the several Lodges of Scotland by way of application for raising a fund to build a new Lodge."

The committee met accordingly, but an obstacle presented itself. The Lodge had for some time been in a state of passive rebellion and defiance of the Grand Lodge, having "for many years neglected to correspond with and pay up the ascertained dues to the Grand Lodge." It was therefore "thought proper to defer such letter or application till that particular was adjusted with the Grand Lodge, for which purpose it is proposed that if Mr George Fraser, Deputy Grand Master,* who is expected North, should cast up, he or some other proper person be waited of and treated with to adjust and settle that point in name of this with the Grand Lodge, which falls to be done previous to any application."

Two years afterwards the new Lodge seems to have been seriously considered.

On the 28th December 1767, "the Master repre-

* George Fraser, Esq., was elected Depute Grand Master of the Freemasons in Scotland on 30th Nov. 1757. He was Deputy Auditor of Excise, and died at Edinburgh, Oct. 12, 1774, having held that office for upwards of fifty years.

6

sented to the meeting that our sister Lodge proposed
to him, and anxiously moved, to have a Lodge
erected and built for the accommodation of both the
bodies, as such a building would not only be a necessary and beneficial ornament, but contribute much
to the encrease of Masonry. That the sum proposed
to execute such a building would come about £150.
That the sister Lodge would apply to their outmost
for contributions to gentlemen who might occasionally be in the place soon, which they would communicate to us, and for their and our exclusive
mutual behooffs, in order to execute this laudable
undertaking, and if the proposal was agreeable to
this meeting, and that the sister Lodge was to appoint
three of their number as a committee, that wee
should name and appoint three to co-operate and
concur with them in the preparative and conclusive
measures for carrying on and finishing so good a
work."

"The foregoing overture having been stated and
reasoned upon at some length, and the votes collected,
the meeting unanimously and chearfully approved of
and agreed to the building such Lodge, and as their
committee for that end they name and appoint the
Right Worshipful [Capt. John Gregor], with Brother
Duncan Fraser and William Cuming, to meet and
concur with the committee of our sister Lodge, hereby authorizeing and impowering our said committee
to concur and contract in and anent every measure
and plan necessary to the carrying on and finishing
so good an undertaking, and engage for and bind the
Lodge to the extent of £75 strg., which sum the
Lodge is by these presents to indemnify and relieve

them. The committee to report to the meeting from 1766 time to time the steps they shall take in course of their proceedings, and that from a regular record to be kept and made by them of their conduct and management in the premises."

So important was the minute of this meeting deemed, that it concludes, "this minute signed at sight, and by appointment of the meeting."

Dec. 13.—"The committee appointed to confer with the St Andrew's Lodge about purchasing an area for building a Lodge, represented that they have not as yet got a proper place. The Lodge continues the powers formerly vested in them."

Nov. 30.—"The St Andrew Lodge sent a deputation, who reported that they are to call in the subscriptions for building the Lodge, and appointed Mr James Clark of London, Mr Lachn. Duff, writer in Edinr., and Mr John Mackintosh, merchant here, to receive the same, in which this Lodge concurs."

How the funds of the Lodge were saved, Dec. 27, 1765. "The petitions given to the meeting, whereof there were many, was severally payed by a collection made by the Brethren from their private pockets, and which as a rule to save the publick funds, the meeting is resolved to abide bye."

The mortcloth, once the pride and privilege of the Brethren, seems at last to have been considered as a burden. On the 26th May 1766 we read :—

"The meeting considering the mort cloaths as an annual burden without any benefit to the Lodge, and

1766 it being overtured by some of the Brethren that the
Trades might be inclined to make a purchase of them,"
a committee are appointed who "are empowered to
treat with the Trades on that subject and to report,"
&c., "on the 24th June."

On that day we learn that "the meeting with the
Trades was delayed as the Convener and Boxmaster
was taken up in adjusting their several accots."

It is not till upwards of eight years afterwards
that we again read of the mortcloth.   On the 27th
December 1774 there is recorded :—

"It was moved and unanimously agreed to, that
the widow of Brother Donald Fraser, squairwright,
should not henceforth receive any fee or salary from
the Lodge for keeping and giving out their mortcloaths, but in lieu thereof that she demand and receive one shilling sterling for each person for whom
the said cloth is given out, and that she is on no account to give out the same without an order from
the Master or Secretary."

On the 6th May 1783, "the Master reported to
the Lodge that he had received one pound one shilling sterling from Hugh Robertson, at the Parks of
Inshes, as mortcloths for his father's and mother's interment, which sum was put into the box."

November 30.—On the 30th November "there
was a visitation from our sister Lodge by Sir Alexr.
M'Donald, Capt. Monro, Dumnagless, &c., who was
kindly entertained."

The Lodge resolved again to change this place of

meeting, and effected an apparently economical ar- 1767
rangement with their future hostess. On the 30th
Nov. 1767 we read—

"The Lodge is to meet at Brother Man's upon
St John's Day next, at 11 o'clock forenoon. Mrs
Man promises to furnish the Brethren in any drink
they call for, and dinner at one shilling per head."

It is difficult to understand, notwithstanding the
terms of the minute, how in those days of heavy
drinking, Mrs Man could profitably implement her
agreement. From the allusion in a former extract
of the year 1761, when absentees were to pay "one
shilling toward payment of the dinner alwise prepared," it seems as if that sum was the cost of the
meal, which, it may be remarked, was liberal
enough, taking into account the relative value of
money then and now. Mrs Man probably calculated
on many members absenting themselves and having
nevertheless to pay their shilling.

On 18th December 1751 the Lodge had declared
that "a procession of the Lodge is looked upon as
idle, and on that account dispensed with." We hear
nothing further as to a procession upon St John's
Day till seventeen years afterwards, when a new
generation of Masons were in power, and urged by
their sister Lodge, the question was again debated,
and the former resolution overturned. On the 20th
Decr. 1768 we read—"Having received a visitation
from our sister Lodge, after they went away, the
Lodge conversed upon the procession next St John's
Day. They continue full powers to the committee
to regulate all matters as they think proper, and

1768 the Brethren are to have their aprons ornamented,
or not, as they please."

Having thus taken the first step, the Lodge
seem to have plunged into dissipation, and had a
procession of unexampled splendour and magnificence.
At all events they were highly pleased with themselves, as appears by the minute of 27th December—

"The Lodge, after regulating their order, proceeded with and joined the sister Lodge in procession.

"The Lodge returned after procession, when they
and our Sister Lodge made a most respectfull and
gentile appearance, with the musick of the Seventh
Regiment from Fort-George," &c., &c.

"The Lodge fixt their plan of going to the play
to-morrow night, when they took one hundred and
fourty half-crown tickets, and are to meet at the
Lodge be four o'clock, so as to proceed therefrom to
the playhouse with musick and flambeaux."

On the 7th January following several of the incidents of the procession were paid, but Brother
Anderson's account was deferred till 2d May 1769,
when—

"Mrs Anderson was paid £5. 14s. 8d. per discharged account, and she is to give the ribbands she
had belonging to the Lodge when demanded."

From this date processions seem to have been
regularly made on St John's Day down to a very
late period.   Occasional notices occur in the minutes
which may be quoted:—

December 15.—" It was moved to the meeting 1769 that in point of decorum the Record Book of the Lodge should in procession be bore on a velvet cushion."

On the 27th December we are informed the " Lodge having regulated their order, proceeded with and joined the sister Lodge in procession, when they made a most respectful and genteel appearance, with the musick of the Twenty-third Regiment from Fort-George, town's musick," &c., &c. The cost of this procession we learn was £6. 2s. 3d. str.

The usual number of members who met upon the festivals of the Lodge may be judged from the minute of 20th Nov. 1769, when the Brethren resolved to meet at Brother Muir's upon St John's Day next, and appoint him to prepare dinner at *two* o'clock for twenty persons.

A case of discipline occurred on the 30th of November 1769. The nature of the offence is not described :—

" Upon a motion to the Chair and the vote put, Angus Shaw was unanimously expelled this Lodge, as being thought unworthy of continuing a member thereof, and was therefore FOR EVER extruded and dismissed accordingly."

On the 10th April 1770 a fine of 6d. for non-attendance was imposed, " from the example of all well-regulated Lodges," and it was resolved that a " third repetition of absence and refusal of paying the mite hereby enacted, shall be good and sufficient foundation and cause for the Lodge taking a more disagreeable resolution."

On the 3d Sept. 1771 this fine was imposed upon five absentees, who were also "peremptorily ordered to attend for the future, that in the event of the disobedience of any of them the conclusion of the said minute may be duly executed against them."—April 17, *vide* new Rules, p. 113.

Five years afterwards, on 25th March 1776, summary sentence was passed on an absentee—the records of the Lodge having no allusion to this offence in the interval.

"The meeting taking into its consideration the frequent non-attendance of John Pearson, agree not to admit him to the Lodge until he pay double quarter pennies for the year, and agree to the minutes of the 7th April 1772."

These minutes are afterwards referred to (p. 112). They chiefly touched an increase of the quarter pennies, on account of the outlay of the Lodge in connection with the proposed new Lodge.

On the 27th December 1781, "The Master and Brethren unanimously voted that all the Brethren who were charged to the meeting and were not present at the election, do, upon their appearing instantly, pay a fine of one shilling sterling over and above all the ordinary dues."

On the 27th December 1784 "upon resolution it was moved, That the Brethren had early this day come to the unanimous resolution that a circular letter should be sent to such of the members as were

absent this day, requiring their attendance upon the 1784
first Tuesday of February next, in order to pay their
arrears, with certification to such as neglect to attend
that day that they shall be struck off the records of
the Lodge."

On the 1st February 1785, it was reported that
letters had been sent to the Brethren who had not
attended the Lodge for some time, and that they
should have been struck off the books; "but the
Lodge, fond of lenient measures, gave them till Lady
Day next to give in answers, with certification." On
Lady Day the absentees got a further reprieve till
"next meeting."

On 24th June 1785 the Brethren met, seemingly
in a very stern mood, for their sentences on the absenting members were prompt and strict. Their
records bear :—

" The Lodge having taking into their consideration the several messages sent to the non-attending
Brethren in write, with their respective answers
thereto, They unanimously resolve that William
Scott, Operative Mason, be struck from the records
of the Lodge and never more from this night be considered as a member of this Lodge, on account of his
insolent answer, vizt., 'That if he did not appear in
writing this night the Lodge might do as they liked'
—and also his being in arrears to the Lodge. 'And
further resolve that Brothers Duncan Grant, Doctor
Robert Grant, Duncan Forbes, and Robert Rodgers
having failed to compear this night, or send sufficient
apologies, be also struck off the Lodge Record, with
this particular exception in their favours, That it
shall be optional to each of them to be reponed by

1785 petition, on or before St John's Day next, and the Lodge appoint them to be served with a double of this minute on or before the first day of August next, with certification.' "

Ou Lady Day 1790, Captain John M'Gregor observed that many of the members of the Lodge gave up attendance, whereby a considerable sum of money was due of arrears, it was resolved that letters should be written to the whole members of the Lodge to attend on the 24th of June next, and then pay or send in their arrears, and unless they do so, all who will be found due four quarter pennies shall be expelled the Lodge.   Further reference will be made to this minute hereafter.

In June 1770 General Oughton, commander of the forces, and Grand Master for Scotland, visited Fort-George, in order to inspect the troops there, and we find the following minutes anent his visit :—

"Inverness, 5th June 1770.—The Master moved to the meeting that his Excellency General Oughton, Grand Master for Scotland, was expected here on his tour reviewing the troops, and that he apprehended it would be proper and dutiful in this Lodge to wait of him.

"The meeting unanimously approve of the Grand Master being waited upon, and the method of doing so being variously stated and the vote put, it carried that it should be by a committee from the body, and the committee appointed are"—nine members are named—"being nine in number, to join the sister Lodge."

"The plan of defraying the expense was reasoned 1770 upon by the meeting, and the committee, to save the publick funds, voluntarily agreed to be each a crown out of their own pockets. The Lodge agrees to indemnify them of their further advance on this necessary occasion."

On the 15th June we read—"His Excellency Major-General Oughton, Grand Master of Scotland, having arrived in town, was waited upon by a joint deputation of both Lodges, and his Excellency was pleased to honour the Lodges with his presence at an entertainment provided for that purpose at the joint expense of both Lodges—the Master of this Lodge being in the chair, the Grand Master refusing to accept."

On the 5th June 1770 the Lodge voted twelve shillings out of the box for the interment of George Nicolson, late Tyler ; and Brother William Cuming was paid seven shillings and sixpence for painting and gilding the truncheons and rods.

The same minute records the interest which the Lodges took in the conduct of public officials, and the sister Lodge of St Andrew has an entry of nearly similar import :—

"The Lodge having taken into consideration how obnoxious Robt. Warrand, the present postmaster, is to them and several others, and how necessary it is that that office should be filled by a man of fair character, and one who possesses the confidence and esteem of his neighbours, resolved and agreed on an application to the Grand Master to have him removed from that employment, and that in conjunction with the sister Lodge."

From the terms of this application to General
Oughton, it appears as if Mr Warrand, the postmaster, was a military man.

In 1770 the Grand Lodge, by advertisement,
called upon the different Lodges throughout the
country to pay their dues to the Grand Secretary,
under threat of calling in their charters. It appears
that our Lodge was among the defaulters. The
Master having observed the advertisement, called
together a committee, which met upon the 23d
October, when—

" The Master represented that he had seen a
publick advertisement from the Grand Lodge signifying and intimating to all the different Lodges in
Scotland, that if these Lodges did not make report
to the Grand Secretary of the members belonging to
and entered in each Lodge, and pay up the ordinary
dues to the Grand Lodge on or before the 12th
Novemr. next, the Grand Lodge would, upon the
30th, call in all charters flowing from them to such
Lodges, and consider the deficients no longer as
collective Lodges of the Grand Lodge."

The committee having reasoned upon the import
of the said advertisement, they propose in the meantime that a letter should be writt to the Grand
Secretary as follows, viz.:—

" Sir,—Having observed your late advertisement
in the publick papers, this Lodge begs leave to inform the Grand Lodge that they have for many
years back preceding St John's Day 1764 been under
the management of Operative Brethren, who were

totally indolent in promoting Masonry or attending 1770
to the interest of the body, which gave occasion to the
Brethren who then and since compose the Lodge
necessarily, and indeed altogether, to shake them
off, since which it may be said they've to a man
decayed and out of time. By reason of this, and
finding matters in such confusion, it has hitherto
defied the Brethren's best purposes of bringing their
funds and matters to such a bearing as they could
wish, particularly in exacting the moiety payable to
the Grand Lodge. Meantime I am desired to send
you enclosed an extract roll of the stated members of
the Lodge, for whom the Lodge are willing to pay
the ordinary dues upon advising of the extent, as we
find no vestige on record that can inform us thereof.

" This Lodge being cordially desirous to maintain
their charter, and merit the protection and countenance of their mother Lodge, you'll be good enough
to favor me with an answer as soon as possible, to be
laid before the Brethren, so as their directions may
be forwarded to a Brother at Edinburgh, and I am,
with esteem, Sir, your most obedt. humble servt.

" P.S.—At same time you'll please send a coppie
of the form of proxy proper to be issued from this
Lodge to a member for representing them in the
Grand Lodge."

We cannot altogether approve of the tone and
sentiments of this letter. Whatever the faults of
the Operative Brethren, their indolence or ignorance
of business, the then members of the Lodge should
have remembered it was to them they were indebted
for carrying on the Old Kilwinning Lodge for upwards of a century, and we may record our gratitude

1770 to the old operatives of Inverness, our predecessors in this, one of the most ancient Lodges in the kingdom.

On the 6th November the Master reported to a meeting of the Lodge the doings of his committee, and that "a letter was wrote to Alexr. M'Dougal, Esq., Grand Secretary, with a list of thirty members to which the said Grand Secretary returned his answer, which was read to the meeting. The dues payable to the Grand Lodge were £4, which sum was that night collected and delivered to Mr Charles M'Intosh, writer in Edinburgh, who was unanimously elected as their proxie to represent this Lodge in the Grand Lodge, and his commission was given him to that effect."

The next minute of interest is one highly to the credit of the Lodge, and shows the care of the Brethren that none but men of honesty and uprightness should belong to their body. The case occurred on 5th February 1771, and is thus recorded :—

"Brother John Collie represented to the chair that John Fraser, messenger, had been entrusted by Neil Beaton, mercht. in Maryburgh, with thirty-one pound one shilling sterling, to be delivered to him, the said John Collie, on account of Mr William Mouat, merchant, Aberdeen, and that he had only paid him £20 of the foresaid sum, and positively declared that he had received no more from Mr Beaton. Brother Collie also presented a letter from Mr Beaton of the 11th Jany currt. advising of his having delivered £31. 1s. to John Fraser before two reputable witnesses ; which being duly considered and the vote put, the said John Fraser was unanimously

expelled this Lodge, as very unworthy of continuing 1771
a member thereof, and was FOR EVER EXTRUDED N.B.
and DISMISSED accordingly ; he having, after first
communing with Brother Collie, acknowledged to
have received the whole sum mentioned by Mr
Beaton in said letter."

This extreme but well merited sentence, as if to
mark their sense of its importance, has the words
"for ever" engrossed in the largest capital text the
lines will allow, and the letters "N.B." added on the
margin.

About three and a half years thereafter, on 30th
November 1774, we read—

"A petition was presented by John Fraser, messenger at Fort-William, humbly craving to be reponed to his privilege as a member of this Lodge, of
which he was deprived by a former minute of the
5th February 1771, And the said petition having
been duly read and considered, this Lodge agreed that
upon the producing a certificate of his worthy and
brotherly behaviour, as a member of our sister Lodge
of Fort-William since his junction with them, the
desire of the said petition should be granted."

On the 7th September 1775, "the Right Worshipful Master presented a letter and certificate from our
sister of Fort-William in favour of John Fraser, late
messenger in this place, now residing at Fort-
William, which having been read and materially
considered, as also the minute in our record of 30th
November last, the Lodge unanimously agreed, and
hereby agree, that the said John Fraser be REIN-

1775   STATED and REPONED to all his privileges as a
Brother Mason of this Lodge, and appoint his certificate as such to be given him, as allso a coppie of this
minute."

Thus the minute of 5th February 1771, with its
" For Ever" in largest capitals, and N.B. in the
margin, was quietly rescinded.

It is probable that General Oughton made a
yearly visit to the North for the inspection of the
troops, as again, in June 1771, we read—

11th June.—" The meeting finding that the
Most Worshipful Grand Master, Lieutenant-General
Oughton, intended to be here to-morrow evening,
unanimously agreed to hold a Lodge in order to receive him, and for that purpose to prepare a proper
and elegant entertainment."

On the 13th the minute, signed " Jas. Adols.
Oughton, G.M.," is—" The Master, Wardens, and
Brethren being present, several instructive charges
and directions were given with regard to Masonry, and
the proper tosses [toasts] drunk and songs sung, &c."

On the same date " It was unanimously agreed
that the Master, Wardens, and a number of the
Brethren, as a committee, should wait of SISTER
Robert Anderson, and return *her* the thanks of the
Lodge for her extraordinary care and trouble in providing and regulating the entertainment in the most
elegant manner," and on the 24th June this matter
is again alluded to.

" The Right Worshipful Master reported to the

meeting that the committee appointed by the former 1771 minute waited of Sister Anderson and returned her the thanks of the Lodge, which was received very kindly."

On 27th Dec. 1771 a particular mark of respect was shown towards the Master, Capt. John Gregor:—

" The Right Worshipful Master having removed from the chair to an adjoining room upon the motion of a Brother, the Lodge unanimously voted their thanks to him for his particular attention to the interest of the body and singular services to the Lodge, and they appoint Brother Robert Anderson to report the same, which was done accordingly."

On the 25th March 1772 we read of a deputation The New received from the sister Lodge, " with proposals to Lodge. this Lodge to accept of a certain share of the purchase they had made from Wm McIntosh, Esq. of Holm, of the two roods of bigging in the East Street, commonly called Cumming's Closs." Two or three visits were interchanged between the Lodges, " but the same business not being effected this night," a committee was appointed to meet with a committee of the sister Lodge, and report their procedure again next meeting."

On the 7th April, accordingly, the Master reported that he and the committee had "mett and communed" with the Master and committee of the sister Lodge, and that they had mutually agreed to be equally concerned in the foresaid purchase, and presented a minute thereof, which was ordered to be engrossed in the sederunt, and of which the tenor follows, viz. :—

"At Inverness the twenty-sixth day of March one thousand seven hundred and seventy-two years. It is contracted, agreed, and finally ended between Major Alex. Duff, late of Col. Morris's Regiment, and present Master of the St Andrew Kilwinning Lodge, Inverness, for himself, and as taking burden upon him for the members of the said Lodge, on the one part, and Capt. John Gregor, late of the Royal Highlanders, and present Master of the Old Kilwinning Lodge, Inverness, for himself, and in like manner taking burden for the members of this last-mentioned Lodge, on the other part, in manner and to the effect following : That is to say, whereas a committee of the said first-mentioned Lodge, with the said Major Alexr. Duff, as Master thereof, have lately purchased from Wm. M'Intosh of Holm, Esq., a stance or area in the East Street of Inverness, which now goes commonly under the designation of Cumming's Land,* at the price of £200 sterling money, payable again the term of Martinmas next to come, with annual rent from Whitsunday also ensuing, and that for the purpose of building a commodious house or tenement on the said area, which it is intended shall not only accommodate the Brethren in proper Lodges, but allso answer the intention of an inn in this place : Wherefore it is agreed upon between the said Major Alexr. Duff and Capt. John Gregor as taken burden upon them for their respective Lodges in manner foresaid, *Primo*, That the said first-mentioned Lodge

---

* It may be well to record the site of this purchase, as probably under this description few of us would recognize the now familiar Lombard Street. The High Street was formerly called the East Street, and Cumming's Close or Land formed one of the outlets to the Black Vennel.

shall contribute all the funds belonging to them preceding this date, together with such subscriptions as
they have already procured, or may hereafter obtain,
and that towards building and finishing the said house
or tenement, in order to accommodate the Brethren
in Lodges and att the same time answer the purpose of an inn in this place. In consideration of
which, *Secundo,* The said Old Kilwinning Lodge is,
in like manner, to contribute all the funds belonging
to them prior to this date, with such subscriptions as
are already procured by them, or which they may
hereafter obtain, for building and finishing the said
house, and thereby answering the purposes above
written: *Tertio,* That, as it is the intention of parties
both the Lodges should from this date be mutually
and equally concerned and have the benefit of the
said purchase and building for the purposes above
mentioned to be raised in the said area, in consequence of the said purchase, so this agreement is to
subsist and continue, aye and untill the said undertaking is compleatly finished, and that the debts
which may be contracted on that account and upon
the joint security of both the Lodges, are fully cleared
off: *Quarto,* That what money or moneys it may
become necessary to borrow for prosecuting and
finishing the above undertaking, now sett on foot,
shall be raised on the joint security of both the
Lodges, and such sum or sums, so raised or borrowed,
shall affect and burden the Lodges equally and proportionally: *Quinto,* That there shall be a room in
the said house or tenement, and first floor thereof,
properly and elegantly furnished, which is to answer
the purpose of an assembly room in this town, and
to accommodate the said St Andrew Kilwinning

1772 Lodge first mentioned in a room for their usual
meetings : *Sexto*, That there shall also be a room in
the said house or tenement properly and sufficiently
furnished, for accommodating in like manner the
Brethren of the said Old Kilwinning Lodge in an
apartment for meeting in, on occasion of their usual
dyets of convening : *Septimo*, That the above room
first mentioned, in regard it is intended, besides the
purposes agreed upon, to answer that of accommodating company upon occasions of publick entertain-
ments in this place, shall therefore on that account
be highly finished : *Octavo*, That in order the undertaking may the more properly and effectually be
carried on, a committee shall be appointed from time
to time by each Lodge till the building is completely
finished. And both parties become bound to extend
these presents in more ample form upon stampt
paper whenever one shall require the other so to do.
And also to implement and perform the premises to
one another under the penalty of £50, &c. In witness whereof they have subscribed this minute, wrote
by Charles Fraser, writer in Inverness, at Inverness,
place, day, month and year of God above written,
before these witnesses, William Chisholm, Esq., doctor of medicine in Inverness; Baillie John M'Intosh,
merchant in Inverness; and the said Charles Fraser,
Capt. William M'Gillivray of Dunmaglass, and Mr
William Cuming, merchant in Inverness (*sic subscri-
bitur*), John Gregor, Alex. Duff, Will. M'Gillivray,
witness; Wm. Chisholm, witness; Willm. Cuming,
witness; Cha. Fraser, witness."

I have given this agreement in extenso, as exhi-
biting the terms of the contract between the two

Lodges and the designs of the proposed Lodge, al- 1772 though the scheme of building in Cumming's Close was not carried out. I have been unable to trace the cause of the giving up of this scheme, but it is probable that the new Lodge on our present site was completed in the form above indicated. I am informed that what is called the testing clause of the preceding document may be of some interest to our legal Brethren, as showing the late period in which a larger number than two witnesses were employed, and also the fact of a witness being mentioned who did not attest the deed.

At the previously quoted meeting of April 7, 1772, the agreement above given was ratified by the Lodge :

"And in token thereof they agree that a minute be insert on the next page, and to be subscribed by each member of this Lodge, to free and relieve the Right Worshipful Master of his engagement in the foresaid purchase."

Accordingly the minute follows, signed by 29 members.

At the same meeting a "subscription paper" was opened for this Lodge, when it is recorded that "all the members present subscribed according to their inclination."

It being now necessary to provide as much funds as possible for the important purposes of the Lodge, the dues of entry, &c., were raised, and the following new orders and regulations were agreed to by the Lodge, and signed by 34 members :—

" That the dues of an entered Apprentice shall

1772 from this time be one pound one shilling sterling
over and above the Grand Lodge dues, and that of
a Fellow-craft and Master Mason ten shillings and
sixpence ster. for each degree, for the benefit of the
publick funds of the Lodge."

These dues were double the old rates.

By the same new regulations, absentees were to
be fined one shilling sterling for each night's absence,
and "such members as do attend, must do so with
that propriety and decorum that becometh Brethren,
or forfeit double quarter pennies for the year;" and
lastly, the quarter pennies were increased from 1s.
4d. to 2s. per annum, " to be paid regularly every
quarter."

There is no further mention of the building of
the new Lodge until the 7th March 1775, when we
read :—

"The Master reported, that upon Wednesday the
first currt. both Lodges had made purchase at the
publick roup before the Magistrates of this burgh of
the area or waste ground consisting of two roods adjacent to the tenement presently possessed by Brother
Robert Rodgers, and that at the neat sum of fifty
pounds sterling payable to the said Magistrates or
their treasurer again the term of Whitsunday next
to come."

"Thereafter there being present the following
Brethren of our sister Lodge, viz., Capt. Alex. Duff,
Master; Capt. Wm. Bannatyne, Mr Hugh Falconar,
Mr Charles Fraser, writer; and Mr Wm. Cuthbert,
mercht., a further purchase was made from Alexr.
Beaton and Mary Williamson his spouse, of the rood

of bigging belonging to them next to the foresaid 1775
area on the south side, for the sum of £52. 10s. sterling, payable again the term of Whitsunday next,
and the sum of five shillings sterling of earnest;
upon which the proper writts of sale were given and
exchanged in publick Lodge, the said Alex. Beaton
and Mary Williamson his spouse being personally
present."

From this date forward there are frequent allusions to the progress of the new buildings and the
various difficulties and troubles into which the Lodges
got, partly from want of funds and partly from changes
of tenants and other causes. But the sister Lodge of
St Andrew, being the more wealthy and influential
of the two, and taking a more leading part in the conduct of the affair, the various steps are more fully de-
tailed in their minutes. I shall therefore leave the
further history of the building of the new Lodge
untl I take up the records of the St Andrew's Lodge.

General Oughton having again visited the North, 1773
he was received by the Brethren with their accustomed respect. On 2d November 1773 it is reported
to the meeting :—

"That according to a previous concert, a deputa-
ton from both Lodges waited on his Excellency
General Oughton on his arrival in town, at that he
was pleased to favor the Brethren with his company
at the Town's Hall upon the 31 May last, where an
elegant entertainment was provided for him at the
joint expense of a committee of both Lodges, and
that his Excellency was pleased to give a suitable
lecture on the occasion."

1773   A singular mark of respect was exhibited by the Lodge towards Captain John Gregor, who had so often worthily occupied the post of Master. On the 27th December 1773 a new list of office-bearers were elected—Mr Duncan Fraser, Master—

"Thereafter the Right Worshipfull, now in the chair, and the whole of the Brethren present, unanimously expressed their satisfaction and approbation of the great attention and application of their late Right Worshipful Master, Capt. John Gregor, to promote the honour and interests of the Lodge during the whole period of his fulling the chair, and in testimony thereof returned him their most cordial thanks, appointing the same to be recorded in the minutes of this day.

"Thereafter the Lodge, in further testimonie of their approbation of the said Capt. John Gregor's services, voted to give him a medal at their expence, the design and value hereof is to be referred to a committee of this Lodge."

1774   "February 1.—A committee appointed are hereby required to carrie into execution the appointment of the Lodge anent the medal voted to be given Capt. John Gregor in the minute of St John's Day last, and to report the same to the Lodge again Lady Day next."

It was only on the 2d May 1775 that the medal was presented to Capt. Gregor. In the minutes of that date we read :—

"Thereafter Brother Duncan Fraser, elected Master St John's Day 1773, did, in terms of the unanimous appointment of the Lodge of that date 1775 and of 1st Feby. 1774, and also of this night, present Capt. John Gregor, our present Right Worshipfull Master" [he had been again elected Master 27th December 1774] "with a gold medal and the best thanks of the Lodge for his past services, and the Lodge hereby orders the Secretary to pay Mr Robt. Anderson for the said medal, and take his receipt for the same."

On the 6th February 1776 the following diploma was further presented to Captain Gregor—

" The Right Worshipfull Master, Wardens, and Brethren presented our late Right Worshipfull Master Capt. John Gregor with a diploma, and best thanks and wishes of the Lodge, of which diploma the tenour follows thus :—

"AND THE DARKNESS COMPREHENDED IT NOT."

"In the East, a place full of light, where reign silence and peace. We, the Master, Wardens, and Brethren of the Old Kilwinning Lodge, No. 8 in the Register of Scotland, do declare, certify, and attest to all men enlightened, spread over the face of the earth, that this our worthy and well beloved Brother, the bearer hereof, Leutt. John Grigor, of the 42d or Royal Highland Regiment, did return from the service of his king and country to this his native place, in the year 1764, and joined our Lodge: and from our knowledge of his great ability and strength in Masonry, was unanimously elected Master, which important chair he filled for ten years with the utmost approbation, during which time he instructed

1776   us in Masonry, tending much to our mutual advantage, increase, and cement in friendship and brotherly love: and in return for his many eminent services, we have, in token of our gratitude, presented him with a gold medal bearing the thanks of the Lodge. And now, being recalled to the service of his king and country, we do most affectionately recommend him to all warranted Lodges and regular worthy Brethren, where Providence may order his lot. Given under our hand and seal, at Inverness, this sixth day of February 1776, and year of Masonry 5776 A.M."

1782   In the minutes of 27th December 1782, notice is taken of a payment of £2. 19s. 1d. to Brother Robert Anderson, which is probably the price of the gold medal made and engraved by him for Captain Gregor.

I may here remark, in passing, that the minutes conclude—" Thereafter the usual songs sung and toasts drunk, the Lodge was decently and orderly shut;" and that the word almost invariably made use of is "tosses" or "toases." Sometimes the expression is varied to "drinking the ordinary healths," and on a few occasions the word "toasts" is used. But the most frequent use is made of "tosses." It is acknowledged that the derivation of the word "toast" is obscure, and many attempts have been made to settle its etymology. Is it probable that it is derived from "a toss of liquor," the old mode of expressing *a glass?* *

In these days of School Boards and compulsory

* French, *tasse:* Scots, tassie.

education, the following minute will be read with
interest :—

"On 2d May 1775, the Master reported that
Provost Chisholm communed with him about giving
the use of the Lodge Room to an English schoolmaster for the purpose of a school, for a twelvemonth
from the term of Whitsunday next, for which he
promised to pay three pounds sterling of rent, and
that we should have the use of the Lodge Room on
all Lodge nights, and the voice being put, the members unanimously agreed to the above proposal, and
impowered the Right Worshipfull to settle with
Provost Chisholm accordingly."

On the 24th June 1775 was admitted as an entered apprentice John Ettles, vintner, the father of
the lady lately deceased, who founded the annual
lectures in connection with the Royal Academy, and
the Ettles Bursary at the University of Aberdeen.

On the 17th January 1776, " the Master observing that the Junior Warden was not properly
cloathed, and upon enquiry being made for the sash
and medal of that office, was informed that they were
in the possession of Brother William Welsh since St
John's Day 1773. Therefore the Master and Brethren appointed the Secretary to call on Brother Welsh
and demand the said sash and medal, with certification to him, if they are not delivered before next
meeting, he will be made liable for the same."

On 6th February 1776 it is entered that the
Junior Warden's sash and medal being found and
delivered to Thomas Young, the present Junior

1776 Warden, the minute of 17th ult. relative thereto is void and null."

The admission of a member "at an occasional meeting" on 23d January 1776 is worthy of quotation :—.

"Donald Cameron was duly received and admitted an entered apprentice, by entreaty of, and a friend to, our worthie Brother, Cap. Forbes of New, who was present."

The New Lodge.

On the 25th March 1776 the foundation-stone of the new Lodge was laid, and the transaction is thus quaintly recorded :—

"Thereafter the Lodge, after regulating their order, went and joined the sister Lodge on the street, in procession, preceded by a band of music, to the Church Street, where the foundation-stone was laid of an eligent new Lodge intended to be built for the use of both Lodges. The Lodges made a most genteel and respectfull appearance. Returned to our respectfull Lodges, and pass'd the day with that friendship and harmony which so remarkably distinguish that ancient and honourable institution."

The accounts of the Lodge were balanced on St Andrew's Day 1776, whereby the sum in hand appeared to be £12. 10s. 11d. The abstract of the accounts is engrossed in the minutes. It extends from 25th March 1770 to 20th January 1776, and commences with a balance in hand on the former date of £86. 1s. 10d. Subscriptions received (apparently for New Lodge), £9. 9s.; and cash received 1776 (apparently ordinary revenue), £47. 7s. 10d. The payments were £84. 14s. 10d. on account of the new building, and £45. 12s. 10d. on account of the Lodge.

On the 7th February 1777 it "was unanimously 1777 agreed upon that no operative mason should be admitted without paying one guinea and the ordinary dues of the Lodge." As a guinea was the ordinary fee on admission paid by all the members, it would seem as if previously the operative masons were admitted at a lower rate.

Upon the 4th of February 1783, "the Master proposed having the flooring of the Fellow-crafts and Master Masons painted and framed, as also a neat box for holding the Mortcloath, arms, and a strong chest for prevesrving and skaithless keeping the three floorings and cushion, together with the sashes and medals of the Lodge; which were unanimously approved of as absolutely necessary. And the meeting empowered the Master to purchase and present them again next meeting, to be paid out of the funds of the Lodge."

From a minute of 7th Octr. 1783 we find that the cost of these articles amounted to £4. 1s. 6½d.

The conduct of the Brethren seems to have been watched with care, both in and out the Lodge, and on 7th October 1783 John Kinnaird, dancing master, was severely censured as follows :—

" Certain information having been laid before the meeting that, in the month of June last, John Kinnaird, dancing master, and a member of this Lodge,

1788 did, in the shop of George Schivez, merchant, before
Mr Kenneth Schivez, and William Grant, residenter
in Inverness, insult Brother Thomas Young with the
most opprobrious names, and the said Brother Young
having been asked by the meeting as to the above
information, and having fully verified the same to
the satisfaction of the Brethren, they all unanimously
resolved, and hereby resolve, that the said John Kinnaird be from this date suspended from being a member of this Lodge, untill he give complete satisfaction
to the body for the above unprovoked assault given
to the said Brother Young."

Thereafter, information being also laid before the
meeting that John Stuart, flax-dresser, and a member
of this Lodge, had been charged by Messrs Shaw and
Son, his masters, with infidelity in the discharge
of the trust committed by them to him, the meeting unanimously resolved, and hereby resolve, that he
be also suspended from being a member till he clear
up his character to the satisfaction of the Lodge.

On the 1st Decr. following, "the minutes of 7th
Octr. last being read to this meeting, they all unanimously approved thereof, and confirmed them, allowing to John Kinnaird and John Stuart till St John's
Day to give in their defences."

On the 27th December 1784, "a letter from John
Kinnaird, dancing master, craving to be re-admitted
to the Lodge, having been read and duly considered, as
also the letter sent him specifying the charge against
him, as formerly minuted, and as yet he has made
no answer satisfactory to the Lodge—Therefore, the
Lodge unanimously resolved and agreed that the sentence of suspension against the said John Kinnaird,

of date 7th October 1783, stand in full force against 1783
him until he gave full satisfaction to the Right Worshipful Master and to the Lodge."

On 27th December 1785 "the Lodge chearfully,
in conjunction with our sister Lodge, appointed to
have a ball on Wednesday, the eleventh January
next, for the encouragement of Brother Lachlan."

I have left till I come to the history of the St
Andrew Lodge the account of the building, furnishing, and letting of the new Lodge, but the following
minute, on the occasion of the completion of the
Lodge, is so complacent that it deserves quotation:—

" On the 14th June 1786, The Right Worshipfull
the Master, Wardens, and Brethren, in a full meeting, for the purpose of examining the state of the
New Inn since the entry of Mr Beverley, duly met
and constitute.

"After the examination of the house, found that
the furniture is most elegant and in taste, and the
service complete, and do approve of the report and
intention of the sister Lodge in having the same inserted in the newspapers, and this Lodge are fully
resolved to give their countenance to Mr Beverley,
according to his merit and attention to the public."

On the 27th December 1786 a new feature ap- Climate of
pears in the minutes, viz., the engrossing therein of Inverness.
the sederunt or list of members present. Meetings
appear to have been regularly held, but there are no
minutes recorded till the 14th December 1787, when
an incidental entry points out the immense improvement that has taken place in the climate of the

1787   Highlands during the last ninety years, arising chiefly
from the extensive drainage, planting, and reclaiming
that has taken place.

On the last date "the Master represented that
owing to a late harvest he was prevented from attending the Brethren upon St Andrew's Day (30th
November.)" Probably our farmers of to-day would
deem a harvest even five weeks earlier a late one.

On the 28th March 1788 nine new aprons were
ordered "to be chosen and prepared" for the officers
of the Lodge.

The usual meeting to be held on St Andrew's
Day was "put off till 3d December on account of
the unfavourable advice of his Majesty's health."
This seems a curious mark of respect. To adjourn
their meeting for three days only!

1789   On the 27th December 1789, a compliment was
paid by the Lodge to two of its members, which the
minutes carefully state is not to be meant as a precedent:—

" It was moved by the Master, and the Brethren
took into consideration the particular circumstances
of two of their Brethren, viz., Robert Man and
Kenneth Mackenzie. The unanimous opinion was
that from their uniform unexceptionable conduct as
Masons, and punctual attendance heretofore, they
should be charged and welcomed at all times to after
meetings; discharged of bygone quarter payments,
and exeemed from future. This compliment the
Lodge do not mean as a precedent."

On the 28th August 1789, the foundation of the
steeple of Inverness was laid. A fuller account of

this interesting event is given in the Records of the 1790
St Andrew Lodge.

On Lady Day 1790, an effort was made to reduce the Lodge expenditure upon the annual meetings. " It was mentioned from the chair that the expense attending the meetings of this Lodge, expended out of the public funds, was universally greater than the funds would admit, and requested of the Lodge to say what is proper to be done. The Lodge, all in one voice, are of opinion, that the expense of dinners and drinks expended therein ought to be paid by the members present, and no part laid out of the public funds except that of the Tylor, and recommends to all future Lodges to pay a strict observance of this resolution; and in order to contribute to this, it is also the resolution of this Lodge that such of the members who generally attend, and fail attending at any regular quarterly Lodge, ought, at their first appearance, to pay a shilling costs, to be applied towards the expenses incurred by the members in the Lodge."

We some time previously referred to a resolution passed on Lady Day 1790, directing letters to be written to all members usually absent and in arrears, to attend upon the 24th June; certifying those who remained absent and were four quarter pennies in arrear that they should be expelled. On the 24th June accordingly, it was reported that the Tyler had delivered letters to those members in the town and neighbourhood, and being called upon, and having given in a list of their names with their answers in writing, whereby it appears that the following persons, viz.:—

8

1790
Duncan Grant, writer.
John Baillie, wright.
William Henderson, bleacher.
William Sharp, stationer.
John Ettles, vintner.
Donald Mackintosh, shipmaster.
William Fraser, writer.
James Blair, musician.
John Gibson, merchant.
William Scott, mason.
Hugh Fraser, messenger.
Alexander Mackenzie, coppersmith.

have treated the several messages sent them by the
Lodge with *contumacy*, and either did not send or refused payment of their arrears.

"The Lodge, therefore, do hereby unanimously
expunge the above-mentioned *persons* from all the
privileges and immunities pertaining thereto. At
same time the Lodge considered that several members resident in the county, 'who have for sometime
absented themselves, and did not send payment of
their quarter pennies, could not make answer to the
letters wrote them, it is hereby agreed that the space
of three months longer from this date be allowed
them to send their answer or payment of their
arrears ; but positively declaring that if they do not
in the time now limited, they should be expunged in
same manner.' "

On the 30th November the Secretary reported
that he had wrote the different members in the

country who have not for a long time attended, and **179**
without their making answer, except Dr Robert
Grant of Dingwall, which they esteemed a good
apology, and with a sense of love and lenity which
is characteristic of Masonry, the Master and Brethren
agreed to give a further time for the absenting members till St John's Day first, for either making their
appearance in this Lodge or sending payment of
their arrears.

On the 27th December 1790, Alexander Mackenzie, coppersmith, Inverness, one of the expunged
members, upon his petition, was again received into
the Lodge, "considering that he faithfully promises
in the future to make every reparation as a Mason."

William Sharp re-admitted of the 16th December
1791.

1791

On the 24th June 1791, James Reed, Inverness,
presented a letter from Mr Simon Fraser, now in
Ireland, a Master Mason of this Lodge, who wishes
to have a diploma of his being so, which was unanimously agreed to be given to him.

It is probable that this was Simon Fraser, ensign
73d Regiment, admitted 29th March 1779.

The minute of St Andrew's Day 1790 concludes
—" The usual toasts being given and songs sung, the
Lodge was decently and orderly shut." There are,
however, some indications which would seem to throw
a doubt upon this statement, the handwriting of the
Secretary, in the progress of the minute, which seems
to have been engrossed at the time, gradually becoming irregular, while the signature of the Master,
"Willm. Cuming," usually bold, distinct, and even
ornamental, is almost a hieroglyphic!

On 27th December 1790 the wages of the Tyler

1790 were raised to £1. 5s. per annum.   At same meeting
a petition from the St Lawrence Lodge of Forres,
praying for aid in building a Lodge in that town,
was remitted to a committee of both Lodges, "to
return such an answer as should be thought proper."
There is, however, no further mention of this petition,
either in the minutes of this or the sister Lodge.

"27th Decr.—After the minute was about being
closed, there was a motion made by Brother Alex.
McDonnell for guarding against the receiving of any
Brother from any other Lodge without a petition
being given in to this Lodge in a full meeting, agreeable to the Rules laid down in the Minute Book,
which was unanimously agreed to."

"Dec. 1st.—After the Lodge was decently and
orderly shut—Thereafter it was recollected that
the deputation recommended to this Lodge that a
deputation of two members from each Lodge should
meet on Saturday next to deliberate upon their joint
interests."

1794   The year 1794 witnessed a great accession of
members to the Lodge, not fewer than seventeen
apprentices having been entered (vide p. $\frac{43}{2}$), and the
whole from the more respectable, or, quoting an expression often previously made use of in these minutes,
from the "genteel and respectfull" classes in Inverness.

On the 3d February 1795 it was recorded that
"a number of the Brethren having sometime ago
expressed a wish that there should be a Master
Mason meeting held monthly, for the purpose of
lecturing for the improvement of the Brethren in
that sublime degree of Masonry; the Right Wor-

shipfull, therefore, in compleyance with the desire of 1795
the Brethren, called the meeting of this night for the
above purpose, to give an opportunity to the Brethren
to consider of the most proper days for fixing such
meetings in future. The Brethren of this meeting
therefore appoint the first Tuesday of every month
for the above purpose.

On the 30th November 1795, a deputation received from the sister Lodge "reported that a number of operative masons in this place had presented a
petition to the sister Lodge similar to the one presented and laid before this Lodge this night, requesting the joint recommendation of both the Lodges in
their favours to the Grand Lodge, in order to obtain
a charter for the purpose of establishing a Lodge in
this place."

This referred probably to the Operative Clachnacuddin, which was established in 1796 and ceased
in 1837.

" And their petition to the Grand Lodge being
laid before both Lodges, signed by twelve of their
number, in order to subjoin the recommendation applyed for by them, the same was done accordingly in
terms of their petitions, and signed by the Right
Worshipfull Masters of both Lodges."

On the 18th October 1796 " there was a full and
compleat Master Mason lecture, including the three
parts of entered Apprentice, Fellow-craft, and Master
Mason, much to the satisfaction and edification of the
Brethren present."

On 30th November 1797, a deputation was received from the sister Lodge, which " suggested that

1797 there might be a propriety in having a procession on
St John's Day first, in order to revive the spirit of
Masonry, which for some time past seems rather to
languish. This meeting having considered the same,
they refer it to the deliberation of a full meeting of
both Lodges, which is hereby appointed to be held at
twelve o'clock on the 2d of December next."

Accordingly, on that day, the Brethren having
met and deliberated, "are of opinion that it may
have a tendency to promote the objects in view.
Therefore, they unanimously agree that a procession
shall take place on next St John's Day, and refer the
direction and ordering of the same to the Standing
Committee of both Lodges."

The order of the procession was regulated as
follows :—

"At eleven o'clock on St John's Day the Old
and New Kilwinning Lodge shall assemble in the
Northern Meeting Rooms. That the procession shall
take place precisely at twelve o'clock through the
different streets in town, and return to the Mason
Inn, when the election of office-bearers in the respective Lodges for the ensuing year shall take place.
That in the procession the Senior Lodge shall take
precedence, as has been usual in this place, and that
such members of the Clachnacuddin Operative Lodge
as incline to join the procession, shall fall into the
rear. That each Lodge shall determine the order in
which its members shall walk. That the dress of the
day shall be black, with white stockings, and aprons
without ornaments. The Treasurer of each Lodge is
directed to order the rods, rules, and battons of both
Lodges be in proper order, the cushions brushed,

squares and battons made up or renewed if neces- 1797
sary, &c."

The following account of the procession, under
date 27th December, may be quoted :—At eleven
o'clock forenoon "The Lodge took into consideration
the regular order of the procession, and having gone
from labour to a repast, they afterwards proceeded to
the Northern Rooms, and from thence to the church,
where they heard an excellent sermon preached by
the Rev. Mr A. Fraser, one of the ministers of Inverness, from the 133d Psalm, ver. —, after which
they proceeded in procession, accompanied by the
sister Lodges, through the different streets in town
to the Lodge—the band playing tunes properly adapt-
ed to the occasion."

At three o'clock the Lodge was recalled from "a
repast to labour," being the annual election of office-
bearers, after which they went to "a repast" again.
At half-past six o'clock "the Lodge being called from
a repast to labour, it was moved by the Past Master
and unanimously agreed to, that the thanks of the
Lodge be delivered by the Master of the Lodge to
the Reverend Mr Fraser for the discourses delivered
to this and sister Lodges this day, and having
honoured them with his company to dinner." *

In 1798 a movement was made for the erection 1798
of a hall for the Grand Lodge, and there was laid
before a meeting of the Lodge, on 27th Dec. 1798, a
letter from the Grand Lodge, dated the 18th Dec.,

* As appears by accounts preserved in the minutes of the
sister Lodge the music was furnished by the band of the
Hopetown Fencibles, who were paid £6. 6s. for their services.

1798 relative to erecting a hall for the Grand Lodge, and soliciting the support of the Lodge as members and individuals. This letter was referred to the Joint Committee of the two Lodges, to determine such sum as they please for the purpose. The Lodge directed a copy of the letter and the minutes of the Committee to be engrossed in their minute book. This, however, was not done, and we are not, therefore, informed of the assistance granted to the Grand Lodge.

1799 On 6th May 1799, the foundation stone of the Northern Infirmary was laid with full Masonic honours. The minutes of the old Lodge give pretty full details of this event, which will be read with some interest—the more so, as there is no account of the proceedings in the minutes of the new Lodge.

On the 3d May, " the Master represented that it was the wish of the Committee for building the Infirmary, and of those interested in that laudable undertaking, that the foundation stone would be laid by this and the sister Lodges on any day that would suit them, and moved that the sense of the Lodge be taken thereon. The Lodge agreed to lay the foundation stone in conjunction with the two sister Lodges on any day the Master would call them together." A committee was appointed to concur with the other Lodges as to the arrangements for the procession.

On the 6th May the Lodge being duly met, and having taken into consideration the order of the procession, it was agreed to proceed as follows :—

1. The Toiler with a drawn sword to precede, followed by the Secretary carrying the Bible on a cushion.

2. The Right Worshipful Master.
3. The Past Masters—two and two.
4. Senior and Junior Wardens—two and two.
5. Treasurer and Past Senior Warden.
6. The Brethren—two and two—according to seniority.
7. The Stewarts taking up the rear, according to the usual order, with their long poles, and at proper places going and throwing arches through which the Lodge was to pass, and thereafter to fall into the rear.

Thereafter the Lodge went to a repast, having no other business, and being by the Master called from a repast to labour, he reported that while at repast, the members of the Lodge proceeded in the order mentioned in the preceding minute to the Northern Hunt Rooms, where they were joined by the sister Lodges, the Saint Andrew Kilwinning and the Clachnacuddin Operative Lodge, from whence they proceeded in procession through the streets of Inverness, followed by the said Lodges according to seniority. That having arrived at the Bridge Street they were preceded by the committee appointed for conducting the Infirmary, and the different Lodges were followed also in procession by the respective Masters of the Academy in their robes, and the students following them and bringing up the rear, to the number of two hundred, and, so accompanied, the Lodge proceeded to the ground where the foundation of the Infirmary was to be laid. That after arriving at the ground the three Lodges formed a circle, and a pathetic prayer having been delivered, suitable to the occasion,

by the Rev. Brother Robert Rose, one of the ministers
of Inverness, and Chairman of the Committee for the
Northern Infirmary, the foundation stone was laid
by the different Right Worshipful Masters of the
said Lodges, assisted by the Brethren, and the Lodges
in their order proceeded three times round the ground
and returned to their respective Lodges, which finished
the business.   Thereafter, the Lodge agreed to dine
promiscuously with as many friends as chose to ac-
company them, and the Lodge was decently and
orderly shut.

On the 23d August 1799 a meeting of the Lodge
was held to take into consideration the Act of Parliament passed for suppression of seditious societies,
&c., whereby Mason Lodges were affected.   The following extracts from minutes of a meeting of the
Grand Lodge of Scotland are engrossed on the 5th
August 1799 :—

"It was stated from the chair that by an Act
passed in the last Session of Parliament, cap. 79, entitled, 'An Act for the more effectual suppression of
Societies established for seditious and treasonable
purposes,' &c., it was *inter alia* declared illegal for
any body of men to require an oath, test, or declaration from their members not authorized by law, but
an express exception was contained therein in favour
of Freemasons, under certain provisions of the following tenour—

"And whereas certain societies have been long
accustomed to be holden in this kingdom, under the
denomination of Lodges of Freemasons, the meetings
whereof have been in great measure directed for

charitable purposes, be it therefore enacted that no- [1799]
thing in this Act shall extend to the meetings of any
such Society or Lodge, which shall before the passing
of this Act have been usually holden under the said
denomination, and in conformity to the Rules prevailed among the said Society of Freemasons.

"Provided always, that this exemption shall not
extend to any such Society, unless two of the members composing the same shall certify upon an oath
(which oath any Justice of the Peace or other magistrate is hereby empowered to administer) that such
Society or Lodge has, before the passing of this Act,
been usually held under the denomination of a Lodge
of Freemasons in this kingdom, which certificate,
duly attested by the magistrate before whom the
same shall be sworn and subscribed by the persons so
certifying, shall within two calendar months after
the passing of this Act be deposited with the Clerk of
the Peace for the county, stewartry, riding, division,
shire, or place where such Society or Lodge have
been held; provided always that this exemption shall
not extend to any such Society or Lodge, unless the
name or denomination thereof, and the usual place
or places, and the time or times of its meetings, and
the names and descriptions of all and every the members thereof, be registered with such Clerk of the
Peace as aforesaid within two months after the passing of this Act, and also on or before the 25th day
of March in every succeeding year.

"And be it enacted that the Clerk of the Peace or
the person acting in his behalf in any such county,
stewartry, riding, division, shire, or place, is hereby
authorized and required to receive such certificate

1799 and make such registry as aforesaid, and to enroll the same among the records of said county, &c., or place, and to lay the same once a year before the General Sessions of the Justices for such county, &c., and that it shall and may be lawful for the said Justices, or for the major part of them, at any of their General Sessions, if they shall so think fit, upon complaint made to them upon oath by any one or more credible persons, that the continuance of the meetings of any such Lodge or Society is likely to be injurious to the public peace and good order, to direct that the meetings of any such Society or Lodge within such county, &c., shall from henceforth be discontinued, and any such meetings held notwithstanding such order of discontinuance, and before the same shall by like authority be revoked, shall be deemed an unlawful combination and confederacy under the provisions of this Act."

Which enactments the Grand Lodge have taken into their most serious consideration, they unanimously agreed that it was their province as the head of the Masonic body in Scotland, from whom all regular Lodges hold their right of meeting by charter, to take effectual steps for enforcing the observance of the law before recited—a law which, as bearing honourable testimony to the purity of their order, and thus silencing the daring breath of calumny, must be duly flattering to the Brethren at large.

They do, therefore, in the first place, most strenuously recommend the instant attention of the whole Lodges of Scotland to the foregoing legislative regulations, by which it will be observed that two essen-

tial requisites are necessary for entitling the Free- 1799
masons of Scotland to hold in future their usual
meetings—

" 1st, That two of the members of each Lodge shall
certify upon oath, before any Justice of the Peace or
other magistrate, that 'The Lodge has before the
passing of the said Act been usually held under the
denomination of a Lodge of Freemasons and in conformity to the Rules prevailing among the Lodges of
Freemasons in this kingdom,' and which affidavit,
certified by the magistrate before whom it is taken,
must be registered with the Sheriff-Clerk of the
county where the particular Lodge holds their meetings, within two calendar months from the 12th of
July last, and

" 2ndly. That one of the presiding Officers of the
Lodge do record with the Sheriff-Clerk within the
same space (1st), The name by which the Lodge is
distinguished; (2d) The place and days of meeting,
and (3d) The names and descriptions (designations)
of the attending members."

And the Grand Lodge, responsible for the regular
conduct of the Masons of Scotland holding of them,
which they are firmly persuaded is almost without
exception entirely consonant to the principles of the
Craft, yet anxious to guard every intrusion in their
ancient and respectable order, or upon her established
and accustomed forms as unanimously resolve—

" 1st. That every Lodge holding of the Grand
Lodge of Scotland shall, within six months from this
date, apply for a certificate from the Grand Lodge,

1799 which certificate shall bear an express renewal of power to hold Masonic meetings under her sanction and authority, and which certificate shall not be granted without production of evidence to the Most Worshipful the Grand Master, his Depute or Substitute, that the Act of Parliament above recited has been literally complied with, and every Lodge which shall not, within the said space, demand and obtain such certificate, shall be expunged from the Grand Roll, have consequently no right thereafter, by her presiding officers or by proxy, to sit or vote at their meetings, and be deprived of all future protection of the Grand Lodge.

" 2do. That the said certificate shall be subscribed by the Grand Master, his Depute or Substitute, and by the Secretary and Clerk for the time, and have the seal of the Grand Lodge appended thereto, for which a fee of five shillings and no more, at the disposal of the Grand Lodge, shall be exacted.

" 3tio. That the said certificate shall be thereafter applied for on or before the 25th day of April 1801, and of every succeeding year, and evidence produced as above mentioned, so long as the said Act is in force, under the same certification of being so expunged from the Roll in case of failure.

" 4to. That no such certificate shall be granted unless all the arrears due to the Grand Lodge be discharged.

"5to. That the names of all the Lodges who have so obtained certificates shall be annually transmitted to one of his Majesty's Principal Secretaries of State and to the Lord Advocate of Scotland.

"6to. That the foregoing resolutions be printed, and copies transmitted to all Lodges throughout

Scotland holding of the Grand Lodge, that none   1799
may pretend ignorance thereof.

"7to. That copies thereof be also transmitted to
his Grace the Duke of Athol and the Right Honourable Henry Dundas, by the Most Worshipful the
Grand Master, and he be requested to take that
opportunity of expressing the grateful sense the
Masons of Scotland entertain of their exertions in
behalf of the craft.

"8vo. That a committee be appointed to wait on
the Lord Advocate with a copy of the said resolutions, and who be instructed to desire his Lordship
that they have a grateful feeling of his Lordship's
kindness for the Masons of Scotland, and will be
ready to listen to any other regulations that to him
may appear proper to be adopted, and the following
committee was accordingly named for that purpose.
The Right Honourable and Most Worshipfull the
Grand Master, the Secretary, and Brother Campbell
of Fairfield.

"9no. That a copy of these resolutions be also
transmitted to the Secretary of the Grand Lodge
of Ancient Freemasons of England.

"And lastly, That the thanks of the Grand Lodge
are justly due to the Right Honourable the Most
Worshipfull Sir James Stirling, Bart., their present
Grand Master, for his constant attention to their interests since his unanimous election to the chair, and
more particularly in his correspondence with Mr
Secretary Dundas during the dependence of the said
bill in Parliament."

At the foresaid meeting of the Lodge, 23d August
1799, it was agreed to—

1799   "That Brother William Welsh, the Past Master, accompanied by any other member who may attend, be requested—

"1. To make out the necessary lists pointed out in the above papers.

"2. To make affidavit thereto and to the description of the Lodge and the times of meetings.

"3. To lodge them with the Clerk to the Peace and record the names of the members with the Sheriff-Clerk or other officer appointed to record the same.

"And also to do what else is required by the said statute and resolution of the Grand Lodge."

On the 30th November 1799 the Master reported that in consequence of the last minutes he complied with the late Act of Parliament, "and he now produces extract of the proceedings had in consequence. The meeting order them to be recorded and thereafter transmitted to the Grand Lodge." Follows copy of proceedings referred to :—

"At Inverness the tenth day of September one thousand seven hundred and ninety-nine years. In presence of Mr James Grant, Justice of Peace Clerk for the county of Inverness, compeared Mr Farquhar Macdonald, Surveyor of the Customs at the Port of Inverness, Master of the Old Kilwinning Lodge of Inverness, Number Eight of Scotland, and presented to the said Mr James Grant, as Clerk foresaid, the certificate and declaration underwritten, that the same might be registered in terms of the Act 39 Geo. III., cap. 79, and the Clerk accordingly records the said certificate and declaration, of which the tenour follows, viz.—At Inverness the fifth day of

September 1799 years, in presence of Thomas Gil- 799
zean, Esq., Sheriff-Substitute and one of the Justices
of the Peace for the county of Inverness, compeared
Mr Farquhar Macdonald, Surveyor of the Customs of
the Port of Inverness, Master of the Old Kilwinning
Lodge of Inverness, Number Eight of Scotland, and
Alexander Macdonell, writer in Inverness, Secretary
of the said Lodge, who being severally solemnly sworn,
examined, and interrogate, depones that the deponents
have been members of the said Lodge for several
years, and have attended the same. That before the
passing of the Act of Parliament entitled, 'An Act
for the more effectual suppression of Societies established for seditious and treasonable purposes,' the
said Lodge, 'The Old Kilwinning Lodge of Inverness, Number Eight of Scotland,' has been usually
held under the denomination of a Lodge of Freemasons, and in conformity to the rules prevailing
among the Lodges of Freemasons in this kingdom. All
which is truth as the deponents shall answer to God.
(Signed) Farqr. Macdonald, Alex. Macdonell, Thos.
Gilzean, J.P.; T. Farquhar Macdonald, Surveyor of
the Customs at the Port of Inverness, Master of the
Old Kilwinning Lodge of Inverness, Number Eight
of Scotland.

"Declares, 1st. That the said Lodge is distin-
guished by the above name and designation. 2nd.
That the Lodge met within the Mason Lodge of
Inverness, and the usual days of meeting are Lady
Day, which holds on the 25th day of March, and
summer St John's, which holds on the 24th day of
June; St Andrew's, which holds on the 30th day of
November, and St John's, which holds on the 27th
day of December, and that when urgent business

9

1779 concerning the craft require it, they meet on other days. 3rdly. That the names and descriptions of the attending members are as follows, viz.:—

1. Mr Farquhar M'Donald, Custom-House, Master.
    Mr William Welsh, tanner, Pastmaster.
    Bailie Dond. Macpherson, Senr. Warden.
    Mr Chas. Jamieson, Junior Warden.
5. Mr Alex. Macdonell, writer, Secretary.
    Mr Alex. Macgillivray, coppersmith, Treasurer.
    Simon Fraser, Esq. of Boblainie, farmer.
    Bailie Thomas Young, fanner or tanner.
    Mr Alex. Macleod, saddler.
10. Mr Andrew Laughlan, Custom-House.
    Mr Jno. Mackenzie, merchant.
    Mr Campbell-Mackintosh, writer.
    Mr Henry Andrews, merchant.
    Mr David Sheriff, Kinmylies, farmer.
15. Mr James Sutor, merchant.
    Mr Peter Macdonald, watchmaker.
    Mr William Grant, postmaster.
    Mr Alex. Murray, merchant.
    Mr John Simpson, merchant.
20. Mr Donald Macpherson, messenger.
    Mr Hugh Cobban, merchant.
    Mr William Chisholm, merchant.
    Mr David Macpherson, farmer.
    Mr Alex. Dallas, saddler.
25. Mr Colin Mackenzie, watchmaker.
    Mr George Urquhart, upholsterer.
    Mr John Urquhart, perfumer.
    Mr William Fraser, vintner.
    Mr William Haig, teacher of English, Academy.
30. Mr William Cumming, land surveyor.

Mr James Cumming, farmer. 1799
32. Mr William Macbean, merchant.
Extracted from the Justice of Peace record by
(Signed)   " JAMES GRANT."

List of new members of the Old Kilwinning Lodge of Inverness, No. 8 of Scotland, since 11th January 1796, to be recorded in the books of the Grand Lodge.

> Alex. Macrae, writer in Inverness.
> William Cuming, miln, Bught.
> Allan Stewart, merchant, Perth.
> Captain Alex. Macpherson, of the 6th Fencible Regiment.
> James Mackintosh, tacksman of Kincraig.
> Andrew Mitchell, tacksman of Aberarder.
> John Macpherson, merchant in Fort-Augustus
> James Cuming, miln-wright, at Bught
> William Macbean, merchant in Inverness.
> Simon Fraser, tacksman of Balloan.
> Andrew Williamson, cabinetmaker in Inverness

The preceding list was sent to the Secretary of the Grand Lodge on 27th December, with advice that their dues had not been paid to the Grand Lodge, but that Coll Macdonald, W.S., would do so upon receipt.

On the 27th December 1800 the Operative Lodge "Clachnacuddin" was called to account for granting deputations for holding lodges :—

" It was reported by the Pastmaster that he had been informed that the Sister Operative Lodge had

1800 been in the practice of giving deputations to some of
their Brethren in the country to admit persons into
their Lodge, the legality and propriety of which he
submitted to this Lodge. The Lodge, considering
that the charge required to be investigated, the
Visiting Brethren to the Sister Lodge were instructed
to communicate the same and report. The Visiting
Brethren having returned, reported that they communicated to the Sister Lodge what was reported by
the Pastmaster, and that the sentiments of that
Lodge were that the practice communicated was not
constitutional, and therefore that a committee from
both Lodges should meet on the subject, and call on
the Master and the other officers of the Operative
Lodge for an explanation, of all which this Lodge
approved, and they gave power to the Standing Committee to do in the business as to them shall appear
proper, and to report their proceedings to the next
meeting."

The succeeding meeting was held on 24th June
1801, when the Master reported that the Standing
Committee, in consequence of the appointment of
the Lodge, had met with the committee of the Sister
Lodge. That a committee from the Operative Lodge
had also attended, when it was represented to them
the impropriety of their conduct, as mentioned in the
minutes of last meeting, and they seeing the matter
in the same light, promised to discontinue such practice in future. They stated as an apology for their
conduct that hitherto they, as other Operative
Lodges, had been in the practice of admitting apprentices by deputation for the accommodation of
those at a distance, but that they would discontinue
the practice for the present.

On the 24th June 1801 Brother William Fraser, 1801 tenant of the house, presented accompts of tradesmen amounting to £25. 12s. 8d. for repairing the injury done to the house in the month of March last by an explosion of gunpowder in the cellars of M'Intosh, Inglis, & Wilson, which affected several other subjects, and moved that this meeting would authorize him " to retain to the above extent the next half-year's rent." The Lodge were of opinion that the company should pay for the damage, and remitted to the Standing Committee to ascertain the value of the same.

On 18th November 1801 the Grand Lodge intimated a division of districts for Provincial Grand Masters, and classed St John's No. 9 instead of No. 8, which produced a remonstrance. The letter from the Grand Lodge, and accompanying regulations, are as follow:—

" Grand Lodge of Scotland,

Edinr., 1st Septemr. 1801.

" R. W. Sir,

" The Grand Lodge of Scotland have long and deeply regretted the few opportunities she has had of communicating with those Lodges holding under her; and anxious to promote the interest and welfare of the craft, have resolved that, in order to afford these Lodges situated at a distance, the benefiting of meeting as Provincial Grand Lodges, which will not only give them an opportunity of establishing a more intimate and friendly intercourse with their sister Lodges, but should any misunderstanding or dispute happen, either amongst members of Lodges,

1801 or between one Lodge and another, these differences may be adjusted with greater ease, and at less expense and inconvenience to all concerned.

"The Grand Lodge have therefore divided the Lodges holding under her into proper districts, and over these districts appointed Provincial Grand Masters, with the usual and accustomed powers.

"A copy of these Lodges, classed into districts, I beg leave to inclose, with a printed copy of the instructions sent to James Brodie of Brodie, Esquire, Provincial Grand Master for the district to which your Lodge belongs, and have to request that due attention may be paid by your Lodge to them, as well as any other regulations that the Provincial Grand Master may find it necessary to adopt.

<blockquote>
"I am, R. W. Sir,
Yours, &c.,
"WILLIAM GUTHRIE, G. Secy.
</blockquote>

"Old Lodge, Inverness."

"REGULATIONS AND INSTRUCTIONS FOR P.G. MASTERS.

I.

"That the Provincial Grand Master shall, with his earliest convenience, assemble and convene at a place most suitable and convenient for all concerned, the respective Lodges in his district, and lay before them his Commission from the Grand Lodge.

II.

"That as it is of the utmost consequence to be accurately informed whether the Lodges holding of the Grand Lodge have literally complied with the requi-

sites of the Act of Parliament, the Provincial Grand 1801
Master is requested particularly to attend that the
Lodges in his district have, in terms of the Act of
Parliament and of the resolutions of the Grand
Lodge (a copy of which accompanies these instruc-
tions) been strictly and literally complied with.

III.

" That the Provincial Grand Master shall visit
and assemble the Lodges in his district, at such
fixed and stated times and places as may be agreed
to him and them progressively, in such centrical
places as may best suit the attendance of the
Brethren of the Lodges under his charge, fourteen days
at least prior to the quarterly communications of the
Grand Lodge, if not four times, at least twice in
every year; the Provincial Grand Master always
giving the respective Lodges due and timeous noti-
fication when and where such meeting or meetings
are to be held.

IV.

" That all complaints, whether by individual
Brethren of Lodges or by one Lodge against another,
shall be given in in writing, and must in the first
place be brought before the Provincial Grand Master
of the district. That he shall immediately, or as
soon thereafter as convenient, convene the Master
and Wardens of all the Lodges in his district, and
lay the complaint before them, when they or the
majority of those present shall investigate the matter,
and give such judgment thereon as may appear to
them just and proper.

V.

" That the Provincial Grand Lodge, called for
determining such complaints, shall consist only of

the Master and Wardens, duly elected by their respective Lodges for the year; the Provincial Grand Master, or, in case of his absence, the Master of the senior Lodge present to be presses and convener; and in all questions brought before them, the majority of votes shall determine the matter.

VI.

"That the Masters and Wardens of the respective Lodges shall not be intitled to have a vote at any of those meetings, till such time as they produce their annual certificate from the Grand Lodge of their having complied with the requisites of the Act of Parliament and resolutions of the Grand Lodge.

VII.

"That should either of the parties be dissatisfied with the judgment pronounced, they may bring it under the review of the Grand Lodge by appeal; or should the Provincial Grand Lodge feel themselves *difficulted*, the Provincial Grand Master may report the case to the Grand Lodge for their opinion and direction.

VIII.

"That in case either of an appeal by the parties, or a report by the Provincial Grand Master, the complaint, with all the other papers and productions, and the proof taken therein, must be transmitted to the Grand Secretary or Grand Clerk on or before the first Monday of February, the first Monday of May, the first Monday of August, or the first Monday of November, these being the regular quarterly communications of the Grand Lodge of Scotland.

IX.

"That the Provincial Grand Master shall make enquiry into the orders and degrees of Masonry practice

in the respective Lodges in his district, and strictly 1801
to prohibit and discharge them from practising any
other degrees than that of St John's Masonary, consisting of Apprentice, Fellow Craft, and Master
Mason, the only three orders sanctioned by the
Grand Lodge of Scotland.

x.

" That the Provincial Grand Master shall make
his Secretary or Clerk keep regular minutes of all
the meetings and proceedings held by him and his
Lodge; and that once in every year—viz., previous
to the quarterly communication in February, the
said Secretary or Clerk shall transmit an abstract of
these proceedings to the Grand Secretary or Grand
Clerk, in order that the same may be laid before the
Grand Lodge ; and in his reports particularly to
specify—1st, The names of those Lodges in the district that are in existence, and have regular and
stated meetings, and have complied with the requisites of the Act of Parliament and regulations of the
Grand Lodge ; and 2ndly, A list of those Lodges
that do not hold regular meetings, the cause of their
discontinuance, and as nearly as possible the time
when they give up holding their meetings, so that
the Grand Lodge may be accurately informed what
Lodges are still in existence, and take such measures
as may appear necessary for striking these dormant
Lodges off the roll of the Grand Lodge.

(Signed)   " JOHN CLARK, Sub-Grand Master.
" Extracted from the books of the Grand Lodge by
(Signed)   " JA. BARTRAM, Grand Clerk."

INVERNESS, ROSS, AND ELGIN.

1802   JAMES BRODIE of Brodie, Esquire, M.P., Provincial
Grand Master.

No. on the Roll.	Names of Lodges.
8	Old Lodge of Inverness.
31	St Andrew's Lodge, Inverness.
38	St John's Op. Lodge, Forres.
47	Fort-William.
49	Kilmalymoack.
57	Cumberland Kilwin., Inverness.
67	Dyke.
100	Fort-George.
104	St Duthus at Tain.
115	Fort-George, Arderseer Point.
135	Fortrose Lodge, Stornoway.
176	Robertson's Lodge, Cromarty.
190	St Lawrence, Forres.
196	Trinity Lodge, Elgin.
257	Rothes Lodge.
259	Operative Clachnacuddin Lodge, Inverness.

On the 14th June 1802 the statutory declaration
was made by the Master and Secretary of the Lodge,
to which was appended the list of attending Members,
which were all engrossed in the minute book.

The list of Members is similar to that already
given (p. 130), with these exceptions. The two following are omitted—

Peter Macdonald, watchmaker.

William Fraser, vintner;

While the new Members are—

James Macdonald, merchant.

Alexr. Falconer, farmer.

Alex. Macrae, surveyor of taxes.

Alex. Smith, merchant.   1802

Simon Fraser of Balloan, farmer.

Andrew Williamson, cabinetmaker.

George Munro, merchant.

Andrew Imray, merchant.

James Lyon, merchant.

Arthur Cooper, writer;

While in the communication to the Grand Lodge,
these following are also mentioned as new Members—

Lieut. Alexr. Shaw, of 36th Foot.

William Jones, of Leith.

On the 24th June 1802 a copperplate card for
summoning the Brethren was presented by the Master
and unanimously approved of by the meeting, and
ordered the payment to be advanced by the Treasurer
when demanded.

11th October 1802. The Master intimates a
communication from the Provincial Grand Master
that he intended soon to visit all the Lodges in his
Province, and the Lodge resolve, in order to give
him a proper reception and to be prepared to receive
him in form, to hold monthly Master Mason meetings.

The next minute book begins with 27th December 1802, and contains on its first pages a full list of
all the Brethren from 1803 till 1836.

In 1804 the Lodge received a circular from the
Grand Lodge regarding the admission of visiting
Brethren, and pointing out that certain persons had
been gaining admission on the pretence of being
Masons, and publishing pamphlets pretending to
divulge the secrets of the Craft, and they direct that

1804 a form of oath be administered, and the parties so admitted shall sign their names in a register to be kept for the purpose :—

" FORM OF OATH.

" I solemnly swear by God, and as I shall answer to God at the Great Day of Judgment, that I was duly entered an Apprentice Mason within the Lodge adhibited to my subscription; and I further solemnly swear by the oath I now take, and the oath that I took when I was so made a Mason, that I shall never reveal any of these secrets of Masonry which I may see or hear in consequence of being admitted a visiting Brother in this Lodge of——————————except to a true Brother, so help me God.

(Signed)   ——————————."

In 1804 James Fraser offered to take the Hotel for a lease of six years, at £100 per annum, which was given to him; but in 1808 he sends in a long petition, viz.:—

"Unto the Right Worshipful the Master, Senior and Junior Wardens, of the Kilwinning and St Andrew's Lodges of Inverness.

" Humbly sheweth,—

"That your memorialist labours under the uncommodious and unsuitable state of the House, and the few bedrooms which are therein, the number being only six, and these in such a ruinous state, that during any storm the water rushes in thro' them. In the course of this season many companies left the house on seeing the state of the bedrooms. Her Grace the '*Dutches*' of Gordon, in presence of the

Honorable Mrs Fraser of Lovat, remonstrated on 1808 the impropriety of the house being in such a state, and declared that she would never enter it again if in the same condition.

"The memorialist, ever since he commenced business here, made it a rule to have an experienced cook from the South country, at the enormous sum of twenty pounds sterling in name of wages, exclusive of paying travelling charges to and from thence, and this grievance and hardship he is necessitated to repeat almost every six months, solely from that want of accommodation for servants in their sleeping apartments. *In fact there is no other in the Lodge for male or female in the capacity but the common scullery.* Indeed, the public have great cause to murmur and complain in a manner that may be, and very probably is, most injurious to the memorialist's interests and reputation as an innkeeper, notwithstanding his indefatigable exertions and outlays to please and gain the approbation of every individual who favours him with their countenance.

"The ruinous state of the bedrooms, in his opinion, arises from the want of harling and other repairs, more obvious to skilful tradesmen than he can describe ; and if such are ordered to inspect and report thereon, your worships will see the propriety, nay necessity, of the present application, and the memorialist humbly hopes such measures will be immediately adopted, as will appear absolutely requisite for the welfare and interest of all concerned.

"Your memorialist flatters himself that a generous public will do him the justice to say that nothing has been wanting on his part to contribute to their comfort and pleasure in all respects, as he trusts will

1808 merit their future patronage and support, and he shall endeavour to continue to do so to the utmost of his power.   " JAS. FRASER.

"Inverness, 30th November 1808."

On the 25th March 1806, the Master laid before the Brethren a letter from the Grand Lodge on the subject of building a hall for their accommodation, and soliciting aid for that undertaking. The Lodge having considered the matter, " they are of opinion that altho' the funds are unable to give any aid to the plan of the Grand Lodge, yet that this Lodge should use their best exertions to promote the interest of the Grand Lodge and accede to their wishes, and for that purpose the Right Worshipful has directed to call the whole members of this Lodge to meet on as early a day as possible, for the purpose of taking this subject into consideration, and to come to a final resolution on the subject."

On the — June 1806, the Lodge took into consideration the " humble application " of Mr Duar, seal engraver, Edinburgh, craving that the Lodge would nominate and appoint him as their delegate to represent them in the Grand Lodge ; and having evidence of his " moral good character and disposition," commissioned him accordingly.

Thereafter it was moved by a Brother, and unanimously approved of, that the Secretary be directed to engross in these minutes the " Patriotick songs composed by Brother William Welsh, once Master of this Lodge, and with which he frequently entertained it, and thereby increased the harmony of Masonry."

The songs are interesting as recording the placing of the " Clachnacutin" Stone in its present position on the Exchange. There are three songs in all, and 1806 they are as follows :—

CLACHNACUTIN.

A song, humbly addressed to the Magistrates, Free Masons, and Clachnacutin Society of Inverness, by their obedient servant, WILLIAM WELSH.

OCCASION OF THE VERSES.

By appointment of the Magistrates, this ancient stone (?) was ordered into an hewn pedestal, but the workman, insensible of the sacred nature of the job, not being a Clachnacutin bairn, instead of fitting the place nicely to receive it, most inconsiderately did proceed with his rude hammer to adapt the stone itself to the place.

"TUNE—Hearts of Oak, &c."

At the time the Omnipotent formed this vast earth,
To ffam'd Clachnacutin was given its birth,
And as He design'd it, distinguish'd regard,
He made it a whinstone, substantial and hard.

Chorus.

When of substance so strong, and existence so long,
  Let each man and woman,
  With ardour uncommon,
Clachnacutin extol in the rapture of song.

Long time on our street this Palladium was left,
No second Ulysses attempted a theft ;
No Edward who brought the old marble from Scone
To Westminster Abbey durst bring off this stone.

No Edward who, &c.

It lay near the cross, but no record so old
How long to inquisitive Pennant has told,
Still near it our lads and our lasses abound,
Tell news, or spread scandal in whisper around.

Still near it our lads, &c.

1806 This whinstone all famous, this rest to the tub,
Has furnished a toast, and given name to a club,
May the club thrive triumphant, humanity's boast,
While countrys abroad are carousing the toast.
   May the club, &c.

But orders were given to encircle this stone,
And a mason instructed to get the work done,
Who thoughtlessly raised the most terrible clamour,
By breaking some knobs of it with his vile hammer.
   Who thoughtlessly, &c.

All ranks were enraged at this sacriledge,
Which seemed so to injure prosperity's pledge,
Racks, axes, ropes, gibbets they instantly order,
He'd better been guilty of treason or murder.
   Racks, axes, &c.

Britannia meantime with fingers most clever,
Had loaded her pockets with every small shiver,
And said if a Blood again pilfer my crown,
The next I'll enrich with gems of this stone.
   She said, &c.

I'll set them in stars for my knights, and aford
This piece for a jewel to young George's sword,
And if any king throw my seal in the river,
This lump shall replace it more precious than ever.
   And if any king, &c.

This whinstone tho' wounded, in fame shall increase,
My island's proud foes it shall frighten to peace,
When Dunean with its lads in battalion appears,
And Inglis brings forward the bold volunteers.
   When Dunean, &c.

And Culloden shall likeways distinguish his name
By leading his men to achievements of fame;
For this stone which gives valour to each Northern
  band—
Strikes terror and dread thro' the foes of my land.
   For this stone, &c.

It fires my brave Gordons, Grants, Frasers, Munros, 1806
My Seaforths and Sinclairs to quell curs't bravos
Who seek my religion and laws to subvert,
To ruin mine isles and stab George to the heart.
   Who seek my religion, &c.

On hearing the Goddess the town was composed;
The club-room was crowded, Freemasons inclosed;
The bowl and the bottle in bumpers went round,
And the rooffs in each house Clachnacutin resound.

    Chorus.

When of substance so strong and existence so long,
   Let each man and woman,
    With ardour uncommon,
Clachnacutin extol in the raptures of song.

Two other songs follow in honour of the volunteers, but their interest is gone very much, as they refer to the presentation of cups, colours, &c.

On the 1st July it was resolved to lay the foun- 1807
dation-stone of the new wooden bridge across the
river opposite the old pier. The procession was
formed in the usual manner, and the foundation-
stone was laid on the north side under the pier next
the Merkinch, on 3d July 1807.

The foundation-stone of an Operative Lodge was 1812
laid. This building is situated on the west side of
Church Street, near the High Church, and is presently occupied by Mr Robert Imray, upholsterer.

19th December. —The Lodge had a procession by
torchlight, passing through the various streets, and
"cheering the families of the office-bearers as they
passed them."

January 12.—The funeral of Mr William Welsh, 1816
Past-Master, was attended by the members of the
Lodge, dressed in black, with crape and weepers,

10

1806 wearing medals, white gloves, and white aprons trimmed with blue; Past-Masters to carry the body from the gate of the Chapel-Yard to the grave. The order of procession is given at length.

The days of meeting were declared to be—Lady Day, 25th March; Summer St John's, 24th June; St Andrew's, 30th November; St John's, 27th December.

St John's Day.—The Rev. Alex. Campbell was re-elected chaplain.

St John's Day.—It was unanimously resolved, on the motion of the R.W.M., that a procession to the High Church of this place, to hear sermon, should take place in future in the forenoon of St John's day annually, before proceeding to the election of office-bearers; that the collection made at the church door upon that occasion should be applied towards the support of indigent Brethren, and those having just claims on the Lodge for aid, in addition to the usual contribution made by the Lodge: and that the sister Lodge of this place be invited to join the procession.

1820   January 10 —A statement of the contributions by the two Lodges towards the erection of the Lodge property was prepared, and the following is the abstract of the proportions so contributed. The statement is given in full. But the abstract is only given here—

The New Lodge (St Andrew's) contributed £646   2   2
The Old Lodge (St John's)   .   579   2   2½
                                    ————————————
        Carry forward   £1225   4   4½

Brought forward .   £1225   4   4½   1820
Subscriptions collected by New
    Lodge 374 13   0
Confiscated Estates   .   .   200   0   0

                 £1799 17   4½

March 28.—The Lodge congratulated Mr Alex. 1823
Campbell, their chaplain, on his being transferred
from his living at Dores to the parish of Croy, and
Mr Campbell, in reply, by a letter engrossed, says—

"That to deserve the good opinion of so many
Brethren known to me for so many years, and dear
to me by so many ties, was of itself a source of no
ordinary satisfaction, but to have received it at a
time when *cruelly* and *causelessly* persecuted and re-
viled by ignorance and fanaticism, showed their
humanity and brotherly love."

December 29.—At a meeting of both Lodges
Brother William Smith, architect, was directed to
make out particular plans of the addition proposed
to be made to the hotel, which proposed additions
are to consist of a new kitchen, scullery, and two
family rooms on the ground floor, a large public
room, water-closet, and bar on the second floor, and
eight bedrooms and two w. closets on the other floors.

April 26.—It was arranged to lay the foundation 1834
stones of the County Buildings and the United
Charities of Inverness Institution (Infant School),
now called "The Observatory;" and on the 2d of
May they were laid, the following Lodges taking
part :—

1834   Fingal Lodge, Dingwall.
         Union Lodge, Inverness, including deputa-
             tions from Nairn.
         Old St John's Kilwinning.

The programme of laying the stone is given in
full :—

The level, plumb, and square are applied by the
Principal Officer, then wine, corn, and oil being
handed he poured them on the stone. The Brethren
clapped hands three times and gave three cheers.

December 27.—It was first proposed to form the
two Lodges into a friendly society for the benefit of
decayed and poor Brethren, and also during severe
sickness under the last Act of Parliament. A committee being formed of the R.W.M., the Senior
Warden, and Secretary, to correspond with the Grand
Lodge on the subject.

1841   March 25.—A report embracing a history and
general view of the property ⌈and state of the titles,
&c., with the view of constituting the Society, was
presented and approved.

The committee consisted of—The Right Worship-
ful Master, Alex. Mactavish; the Treasurer, John
Ferguson; Brothers Mitchell, James Suter, jun.;
John Cook Gordon, Thomas Ross, and the Secretary.
Brother Mitchell to be Convener.

The property was then valued at 14
    years purchase, of £230 yearly rent . £3200
Amount of debt and annuity after de-
    duction of interest   .   .   . 1450
                                          ———
        Net value of property   .   . £1770

July 1846.—The foundation stone of new jail 1846
laid with Masonic honors.

The St John and St Andrew's Lodges having
united, and the Friendly Society established, nothing
of particular interest occurs up till this date.

The following are the names of the Office-bearers
of the Society till 1875 :—

Society formed 27th December 1842.
John Thomson, President and Manager.
John Ferguson, Treasurer.
John Cook Gordon, Secretary.
Continued till 1845, when
Alexander Cumming was elected President and
Manager.
John Ferguson, Treasurer.
David Prophet, Secretary.

1846.
Thomas Ross, President and Manager.
John Ferguson, Treasurer.
David Prophet, Secretary.

1848.
Thomas Ross, President and Manager.
Archibald Tait, Treasurer.
David Prophet, Secretary.

1849.
William Simpson, President and Manager.
Archibald Tait, Treasurer.
D. Prophet, Secretary.

1855.
William Simpson, President and Manager.
Archibald Tait, Treasurer.
William Ross Grant, Secretary.

1869.

Andrew Dougall, President and Manager.
Archibald Tait, Treasurer.
Wm. Ross Grant, Secretary.

1873.

Andrew Dougall, President and Manager.
Wm. Ross Grant, Treasurer and Secretary.

ST ANDREW'S KILWINNING, INVERNESS.

This Lodge seems to have been in existence pre- 1735 vious to 21st March 1735.

The oldest Minute Book extant of this Lodge commences 6th January 1747-8, the previous books and records of the Lodge having been lost during the insurrection of 1745.

From some detached papers which I have obtained I have been able to collect some memoranda of interest before that date.

From a cash account, "The Master and Clerk of the Kilwinning Lodge of Inverness with their Box from Si John's day 1736 to do. 1737," we learn that Lachlan Mackintosh was then Master, and John Taylor Clerk. It was approved on 4 Jany. 1737 by William Duff, Pastmaster, and Henry Rose of Merkness, and Angus M'Intosh, merchant, "Wardens for this right apointed by the Master." To the signatures of Lachlan Mackintosh and Angus Mackintosh the years of their official appointments are subjoined.

In this account is a statement of sums paid for

1736   jewels, locks, keys, ribbons, and other necessities, with postage of sums sent south, also for the cost of correspondence in connection with the election of ye Grandmastership. There is also an entry, as paid Robt. Arnat for 12 trowels and 9 hammers. Also a book of constitution.

1737   In 1737 the same Lachlan Mackintosh, merchant in Inverness, appears to have been Master, there is at all events a printed letter from the Grand Lodge, 17th February 1737, addressed to him.

     A communication from the Grand Lodge of 29th August 1739, addressed " To William Duff of Kellymure, Esq., to the care of the Postmaster of Inverness," requests, among other matters, to be informed " what proportion of £100 sterling the Grand Lodge had undertaken to pay in ten years to the building of the Royal Infirmary of Edinburgh," the Lodge was willing to contribute. A draft of the minutes of a meeting held on 29th September 1739 is on the back of this letter, by which it appears that the Lodge " will contribute a guinea yearly for nine years." From the sederunt we learn that Evan Baillie (of Abriachan) was Master, Mr John Shaw and Andrew Monro, Wardens. The names of a few of the members on the sederunt, and jotted on the back, may be of interest :—Major Chisholm Glenmoriston, Inches, Mr Inglis, Captain Bannatyne, William Fraser, Writer to the Signet, Mr Wm. Duff (of Muirton), Duncan Forbes, &c.

     Down to the year 1739 this Lodge had no distinct name, which was displeasing to the Grand Lodge. A letter from Sir George Mackenzie of Granville, dated Edr. November 15, 1739, says, " You must condescend on the name you will for the future be called

by; you are now called in the Grand Lodge by the 1739
name of New Inverness; as this name seemed disagreeable to most of our Lodge, you assume any
other, the name of any saint—St Andrew or Mary,
Solomon's Lodge or Hiram's Lodge or any other."
He also proposes to get made and sent by the first
occasion a chair for the Master.

There is a scroll minute preserved of a Lodge
held 27th November 1739, " in John Taylor's house
be 6 in ye evening," wherein Sir Georg: Mackenzie's
letter was considered.   The meeting appears to have
included all the Members of the Lodge, and among
others present were Evan Baillie of Abriachan,
Master; Angus Mackintosh, merchant, Senior Warden; John Shaw, merchant, Junior Warden; Collector George Colvill, late Master; William Duff
of Kilmuir; Major Caulfield, John Baillie, Torbreck;
James Sutherland of Kinstery; ⸺ Fraser of Fairfield; Lieut. Dougal Stewart, the Laird of Mackleod,
Lieut. Charles Baillie, &c., &c.   It was resolved by
unanimous consent that the designation of this Lodge
be in their charter, " St Andrew, Inverness."   The
Lodge also resolved to order a chair for the Master,
and that the Master write to Edinburgh for jewels
for ye Secretary and Treasurer.   There was to be a
procession on St John's day in the usual form, and
" a ball, St John's day, for the ladies :" presumably
also a banquet among the Brethren, as it was further
resolved, "That the house be obliged to furnish a
large table, fit to contain 20 sitters, again St John's
day."   From the subsequent loss of the principal
Minute Book, the preservation of this document fixing the exact date of the designation of the Lodge is
very interesting.

1739   "Coppies" of the Bye-Laws of the Greenock Lodge having been procured, they were read at this meeting, and the copy is still in existence and is docqueted amongst the papers of the Lodge, and contains a number of quaint and useful rules:—

Number 19 is remarkable.—" No Member of this Lodge shall employ any operative mason in any buildings of his own, or others that he may have any directing off, unless such operative mason has been entered in, and continues to be, member of a regular Lodge, under the severest penalties the craft can inflict. The Brethren of this Lodge being preferable in the first place, and those of Drummond Kilwinning, from Greenock, in the 2d place."

" No. 22.—The Lodge shall be regularly closed at ten o'clock at furthest."

There is now a hiatus of several years. The Minute Book commences with a Lodge held on 6th January 1747-8, at John Baillie's house. The members present included Daniel Barbour of Aldowrie, Master; William Duff of Muirton; Collector Colvill, and Mr Evan Baillie, late Master; Alex. Mackenzie of Fairburn; James Sutherland of Kinstery; Doctor William Chisholm, &c. The Minute recording the loss of the previous Minute Books and Records follows :—

" The distresses and confusions which have happened in the country having interrupted any meeting of this Lodge since St John's Day 1745, when the said Daniel Barbour was chosen Master, the Members did enquire at their Treasurer for their charter,

records, jewels, utensils, and cash; and he reported 1748
to them that when the Duke of Cumberland and the
army came to this place, the room of his house, which
was our ordinary Lodge, became the guard-room of
the orderly serjeant; and that all the particulars
mentioned were destroyed or carryed off, except the
charter, which he saved by accident, and which he
layed before the Lodge.

"The Lodge thinking of this with concern as a
calamity and loss which they cannot remeid, did proceed to elect the proper officers for this year:—

"Collector Colvill, Master; Evan Baillie, Senior
Warden; William Chisholm, Junior Warden; John
Taylor, Treasurer; and William Baillie, Clerk."

At the same Lodge, "James Farquarson of In-
vercauld, Esq., an itinerant Brother," was received
as a Member; and Lts. Alexander Mackenzie, Wm.
Baillie, and James Baillie, all of Drumlanrig's Regiment, were admitted as Prentices and Members of
the Lodge. "Thereafter, the Members agreed that a
select number of gentlemen and ladies be invited here
to pass the evening and dance, Friday next, at six
o'clock."

"It was agreed that a letter should be wrote to Dec. 29, 1748
our Brother Montgomery at Glasgow, to desire he
would send what Regulations and By-Laws as would
be proper for this Lodge." Here follows letter referred to :—

"Sir—Among the distresses and confusion that
happened to us by the rebellion, the affairs of our
Lodge having been neglected and our meetings inter-

1748 rupted for a considerable time, our Treasurer has lately informed us that while the King's army was here, the chest was broke open, and everything belonging to the Lodge carried off except the charter.

"What we most regret is the loss of our records, wherein we had many good regulations, and the satisfaction of a long list of worthy members subscribing.

"In these circumstances the Lodge, considering how much they have formerly been obliged to your assistance in establishing these rules, have put it on me, as the present Master, to apply to you, in their name, that you would favour us with such regulations and by-laws as are proper for our Lodge, of which you know the situation.

"The Lodge offer you their hearty compliments, and expecting your answer as soon as your conveniency will allow,—I remain, sir, your most hble. servt. and afft. Brother, A. C.

"Inverness, 2d February 1748-9."

1749   April 4.   Mr Alexander Duff of Cubin and Doctor John Mackintosh of Barrel's Regiment entered Prentices and Members.

"Thereafter our Brother Montgomery's letter of the 1st March last to the Master containing General Rules and Regulations for a Lodge of Free Masons being read and approven of, the same was ordered to be engrossed so as to be signed by the members present and all future intrants.

The "General Rules and Regulations" referred to are accordingly engrossed in the first two pages of the Minute Book. They number 16 in all, but the following are those only that require notice :—

" 1. The Master is to congregat' the Lodge when 1749 and where he pleases.

" 8-9. That no man can be made a member of the Lodge but by petitioning. That no petition be received on any occasion whatsoever but by balloting, and if there is one single No, such petitioner cannot be received, and this has been always reckoned absolutely necessary to maintain the peace, unity, and harmony of the Lodge, because it may happen that one member may have very strong reasons for not admitting a petitioner, which he does not incline to tell.

" 12. Every Brother that emitting an oath in the Lodge is to pay sixpence sterl., which is to be put into the poor's box.

" 15. If the Master shall so farr misbehave himself as to render himself unworthy the subjection of the Lodge, he is to be treated by a new regulation, no Master in this ancient Society having ever misbehaved so far as to render such a regulation necessary.

" 16. The rules and regulations to be read at every meeting."

The signatures to the Rules number 158. Contrary to the custom which was deemed fashionable half-a-century ago, *every one of them* is distinct and legible. The Members are chiefly the proprietors in the county and officers of regiments stationed in the neighbourhood.

" Nov. 20. Doctor Chisholm and *The Moderotor* (?), Wardens. The Members present sign'd the Regulations. Order'd to purchase silver badges for

1749   the Master, late Master, and the two Wardens; with
square, compass, and other furniture for the Lodge."

" Dec. 19.   Alex. Angus being admitted an Entered Prentice and Free Mason, was appointed Tyler
of this Lodge, and was paid half-a-crown for summoning this Lodge.   The jewels, and other necessarys,
being provided, the charge thereof, amounting to one
pound fifteen shillings and sevenpence stg., was paid
by the Treasurer."   The receipt for part of the fur-
nishings is preserved, and the prices are given as a
comparison with jewellers' charges in the present
day:—

> " To the silver of the Mason's Jewells, weigh-
>   ting 2 oz. 2 drs., at 5s. 4d. per   £0 11   4
> " To Workmanship and Engrav-
>   ing   -   -   -   -   0 16   0
> " To the King's dutie   -   -   0   1   1
>   _____
>   £1   8   5"

" Dec. 27.   Andrew Monro, Master ; Brothers
Baillie and Chisholm, Wardens, and Brother Baillie
as Treasurer."   The office-bearers from this date are
continued consecutively at end of these Notes.

1750   " July 5. The Lodge held upon this date was apparently for the admission of Governor Caulfield, the
sole entry being—

> " The Lodge being opened, our Brother Caulfield
> sign'd the Regulations, and the Poor's Box was put
> about for the first time.   The next Lodge to be on
> St Andrew's day."

Suspicions appear to have arisen as to the story Dec. 18, 1750
told by Treasurer Taylor of the loss of the money
and jewels of the Lodge during the Rebellion, for
" All the Members to be summoned to meet 'twixt
11 and 12 in the forenoon [St John's day next] :
and the Tyler is to charge Brother Taylor peremptorily to attend, that he may be further examined
touching the loss of the money, jewels, and records
of the Lodge, which were in his keeping. The meeting on St John's day took place accordingly, and
there was a large attendance of members. Brother
Taylor, however, did not appear, nor is the matter
again alluded to.

October 1. The Lodge taking into consideration 1751
that, notwithstanding the Regulations and Minute
of the 27th March 1750, several Members in and
near the town do absent from the Lodge without
sending an apology, particularly Brothers Baillie and
Knowles, from this meeting, they are hereby fined in
terms of the Regulations."

November 30. "Brother Knowles was excused
his none-attendance at last meeting, he being out of
town."

December 20. Among the petitions for charity
presented at the Lodge held this day, was one from
George M'Gillican (or, as his name is variously spelt,
M'Killican), surgeon in Inverness, to whom was
alloted 10s., and a like sum to Mrs Macdonald of
Gelloway. Both of these names appear for many
consecutive years. The charity was distributed on
each St John's day.

Among the loose papers is a document pertaining 1752
to this year, being a statement of the accounts with
the six Incorporated Trades, from Whitsunday 1749,

1752 to Whitsunday 1752. Some of these items appear worthy of transcript.

Paid in a Meeting when writing a letter to Mr M'Bain . .	£0	3	6
To Mr Campabel at Daviot for the building an timber bridge on the water of Nairn. . .	1	1	0
To cash spent whine the stent was taken off the house . .	0	4	0
To cash paid for the bell . .	0	18	0
To David Dunbar for a tunge to the bell	0	8	0
To cash given the men that went out with the bell	0	6	0
By cash to James Fraser, smith, for hooks and hold-fasts to the Lady Drummuir's coat of arms .	0	3	0
To cash for a boll lyme to the Trades House	0	0	7
To cash spent with Colquhoun when receiving his rent . . .	0	1	2
To cash paid for the carriage of the dead	1	1	0

The items indefinitely entered " cash spent," speak for themselves, being incurred when payments of money were received. The important bell is thus referred to in the discharge annexed to the account—" The Trades hereby declares that they will maintain the hand-bell to the Masons as they doe for themselves, and this is to be signed by Alex. Frazer, Convener for the Trades; and John Dunbar, with Donald M'Pherson, box-master to the Mason

Lodge of Inverness, for the Masons, and that before 1758
these witnesses," &c.

June 27. The Lodge adopt measures necessary
in consequence of a change in their landlady.—

"The Lodge being informed that Mrs Baillie,
Land Lady of this house, where the Lodge has been
held for some years, is upon the eve of removing,
and that her successor is a stranger to this place, the
Lodge direct the Clerk to comitt the care of their
locked box and, the other utensils belonging to the
Lodge in this house, to the Land Lady who comes to
possess it, and to request of her to keep them in a
secure place till it be determined when and where
to congregate the next Lodge."

Dec. 27. Charity granted to the poor in the
prison of Inverness, 4s.

Nov. 30. "A motion being made by the Master 1759
that a neglect had happened in not offering Brother
Colvill the thanks of the Lodge for a present made
them of a parcel of Masonic glasses; they offered their
compliments, with an apology for not having done it
at the time the present was made."

These (or the glasses presented by Mr Falconer
in 1762, or Brother John Mackintosh in 1786) glasses
are still (1877) preserved in the Lodge and annually
used by the Brethren at their dinner on St John's
night. They are of the plain, old-fashioned pattern,
having bottoms about $\frac{3}{8}$ of an inch thick, and with
thick funnel-shaped stems gradually widening to the
top. They hold about one-half the quantity of the

11

1759 modern wine glasses.   The name of the Lodge is engraved on them, both St John's and St Andrew's.

Dec. 30. "The Master, Wardens, and Brethren
presented William Duff, Esquire, their most respectfull compliments, for a present made them by him,
of a sword for the use of the Lodge.

1760   On 27th December 1760, the Lodge had accumu-
lated, after defraying their expenses and providing
for the usual charities, the balance of £10. 6s.   A
meeting was directed for next Lady-day.   Of this
no record exists, but from the following minute it
appears that they had expended their large balance
in a ball :—

1761   December 28.   "The 19th day of October last
a ball was given by the Lodge, when James Gordon,
Treasurer, was ordered to advance the ten pound six
shillings of ballance in his hands at St John's day
1760, to be applyed towards defraying the extraordinary charge of that entertainment; so that the balance
of the day's receipt, after paying the Tyler five shillings, is a one pound fourteen and sixpence."

1762   Sept. 4.   "The Right Worshipfull Master having intimated to the Members present that Mr Hugh
Falconar had imported six dozen glasses, which were
delivered him for the use of the Lodge : That he had
accordingly sent two dozen of them to Mrs Mackin-
non's.   Upon which it was unanimously resolved by
the company that Mr Falconar, who was present,
should have their thanks, and the same was accordingly presented."

Dec. 26. "It was moved in the Lodge, that as

St John's day interferes with the time in which a 1764
number of our Brethren have companys at their
houses, that therefore, for the increase of our Lodge,
and in order to obviate any excuse, our Lodge orders
that a generall meeting shall hold on St Michaelday's
day, and that in order to concert what's proper to be
done for the rest of that season."

The following suggestive entry occurs, but as
there is no previous entry regarding the matter complained of, we must be content to guess at the events
which called for the minute of censure.

Jany. 4. "The Lodge being formed as usual, and 1766
having considered the complaint entered by Brother
Grant against Brother Robertson, and Brother Ro- Arthur Robertson's defences, are unanimously of opinion,—That bertson of
Brother Robertson do ask pardon of the Lodge, and Inshes
particularly of Brothers Grant, McGillivray, and
McIntosh, being the Members then present, and is
to be reprimanded for his conduct after the Lodge
was closed St John's day, and cautioned for his Dec. 27, 1765
behaviour in time to come, and is to satisfy Miss
McThomson for her loss that night in christill shell
work. After the above determination, Brother Robertson was called upon, and he comply'd therewith."

Whether from Inches's exploits on St John's
day 1765 or not, it was not till June 1770 that he
was raised to the degree of a Master Mason.

Dec. 20. "The Members present having taken 1766
notice that there was no Lodge St Andrew's day, by
reason that so many Members were necessarily out

1766   of town, and that now they have changed the quarters for keeping the Lodge, they names Mrs Mc-
Kenzie's as their quarters* for the ensuing year, and
name Capt. Alexr. Fraser and Alexr. McIntosh as
stewards, and recommend to them to provide a proper entertainment for St John's day, to meet be
twelve o'clock."

1767   Dec. 28.   "In the evening a deputation was sent
to our Sister Lodge and the compliments returned,
who reported That at a communing betwixt some of
the Brethren of this Lodge and our Sister's Lodge,
it was suggested that it would be beneficial for both
the Lodges to have a Lodge built for their mutual
accommodation : That in consequence of the above
communing our Sister's Lodge had made a minute
appointing a committee, vesting them with full powers
for that purpose—Therefore, this Lodge name as their
committee, the Right Worshipful Master, Wm. Chis-
olme, late Mr., and Hugh Falconar, Senior Warden, as
the committee to meet with our Sister's Lodge committee, and to report to the Lodge the resolution of
the committee without putting any of the resolutions
into execution."

1768   Dec. 27.   After the transaction of ordinary business (and election of office-bearers) the minute pro-
ceeds—"When the Lodge was turned to a repast,
and the Members, in conjunction with our Sister
Lodge, proceeded to the procession, and upon returning therefrom the Lodge was again formed in
the usuall manner, and about four o'clock in the
evening a deputation was sent with compliments to

* The strong infusion of the military element in the Lodge
may be noticed from the use of the term "Quarters" for
inn or Lodge Room.

our Sister Lodge, and by them returned in like 1768 manner to this Lodge. Again the Lodge was turn'd to a repast, and continued in that manner during the time of the ball and the lady's stay, and after their departure, the Lodge was closed, and the Brethern desir'd to conveen here be ffour o'clock to-morrow evening."

Dec. 28. At four o'clock in the evening, after transaction of business, " The Lodge was turned to a repast, and after proceeding to, and returning from, the play, in conjunction with our Sister Lodge, the Lodge was again formed, and closed in the usuall manner."

Feb. 10. " It being moved that, in consequence of 1769 an appointment of the Lodge, the Right Worshipful and the Secretary had wrote to Brother Lachlan Duff at Edinr., to send here the form of a diploma and different floorings for the Lodge, and as now the Lodge is informed that Brother Duncan Grant, of our Sister Lodge, is going soon to Edinburgh, they recommend to the Secretary to wait of him and desire that he should call on said Brother Duff, to settle with him the most expeditious way of transmitting the above articles here."

" The Secretary further reported that . . . particularly Mr Kenneth M'Kenzie, younger of Redcastle, who was admitted St Andrew's day 1767, and altho' many meetings since that period have happened of the Brethren, to which he was regularly cited, the Lodge now having taken his neglect into consideration, they fined Brother M'Kenzie in ten shillings sterling, . . , at the same time to notify to him that the Lodge requires his attendance at next meeting."

Nov. 30. "The Brethren having taken into consideration the inconvenience they at present labour under by the want of a proper Lodge Room, and how much it would advance the interests of Masonry in this place to put the scheme of building a house for that purpose (which they have had for some time in view) into immediate execution, and it being absolutely necessary for that purpose to call in the subscriptions of the Brethren, and *others* whose regard for the craft has already led them to favour the design, they do appoint Brother James Clark, of London, and Brother Lachlan Duff, of Edinburgh, their agents for having the different sums subscribed by those who live in or near these places, and that they do transmit the same to Brother John Mackintosh, the present Treasurer of the Lodge, who is fixed on as the Receiver here and centre of all the remittances, with full powers to correspond and grant receipts in name of the Lodge.

"It was afterwards proposed by the Right Worshipfull that the sense of the Brethren present might be taken with regard to a ball and procession on the ensuing St John's day, both which were unanimously agreed to, and a deputation in form having been sent to the Sister Lodge, they reported the preceding resolutions with regard to the subscriptions, ball, and procession, which were approved."

December 15. A committee was appointed for meeting with the committee of our Sister Lodge to concert measures as to the procession St John's day, and also to conduct matters with regard to the ball.

"Major Alexander Duff, Mr William Cuthbert, and Arthur Robertson of Inches being in town, and

having sent no sufficient excuse, tho' summond, they 1789
were find in the sum of half-a-crown each."

Dec. 27. "Then the Lodge was dismissed to a
repast, and proceeded in a procession with the Sister
Lodge . . . . thereafter the Lodge was dismissed to
a repast, and continued so during the ball and supper, and after the departure of the ladies the Lodge
was closed."

"A particular accot. of expences of the procession" lies before us. There was a dinner for eight
persons, which cost 5s. 4d.—8d. each, while the
liquids swelled the bill to £1. 5s. 10d., including

22 bottles porter	-	-	-	7s	4d
8 pints of beer	-	-	-	2	8
(These must have been Scotch pints.)					
6 bottles of punch	-	-	-	6	0
4 bottles of whiskey punch		-	-	2	0
1 bottle of whiskey -		-	-	1	4
Brandy and cinnamon		-	-	1	2

The military, or, as it is called, "the Fort" music
cost £2. 2s. 6d., and the town music, 11s. For
gloves and aprons to the music and toilers, 11s. 2d.
One entry is curious: "For the mortcloath keeper
for the cloath and cusheon frame, 1s. 6d." The
whole expenses were £6. 2s. 3d.

Dec. 28. "The bill for the expence of yesterday
was called for and paid." (This was a separate account from the preceding.) "The Treasurer was
ordered to pay eighteen shillings for 2 dozen of
aprons, and ten shillings for gloves, to the band of
musick, out of the funds of the Lodge."

1770   June 5. "The Right Worshipful having informed
the Lodge that his Excellency General Oughton,
Grand Master in Scotland, was expected soon in
town, it was resolved that immediately on his arrival
a committee of this Lodge should wait on his Excellency, with the committee of the Sister Lodge, and
request his presence at an entertainment to be provided at the joint expence of the Lodges."

The Brethren having taken into consideration
" how obnoxious Robert Warrand, the present postmaster, is to them and the publick, and how necessary
it is that that office should be filled by a man of fair
character and who posses the confidence of his neighbours, resolv'd on an application to the Grand Master
for his interest to have him remov'd from that employment; and the above resolutions having been reported to the Sister Lodge by a deputation in due form,
they were approved of, and unanimously agreed to."

June. " Being joined by the Sister Lodge, a
committee of both Lodges waited upon his Excellency Major-Genl. Oughton, Grand Master for Scotland, and his Excellency was pleased to honour the
Lodges with his presence at an entertainment, provided for the purpose, where he took the chair."

Dec. 27. " The Lodge then dismissed to a repast, and continued so during dinner and the whole
evening, and at six o'clock the Brethren went in a
procession to the Town Hall, where a ball was given
to the Ladies, and a supper thereafter."

1771   June 13. " After forming the Lodge, as usuall,
his Excellency Lieut-General Oughton, Grand Master

for Scotland, was pleased to honour the Lodge with 1717
his presence, took the chair, *and gave a charge to
the Lodge.*"

The preceding is the whole minutes of June 13.
It is signed by "Jas. Adols. Oughton, G.M." Short
as it is, he made three corrections in it, one as to his
title, one grammatical, and an addition. His alterations are underlined with red ink.

Nov. 30. "It was proposed in the Lodge and
agreed to, that on St John's day there would be a
ball, and, in order to prevent any mistake or disorder,
that each member that resolved to be present that
day, or join in the expence of the ball, should each
of them have one ticket to be given a lady, and no
more, the name of which lady each member is to
give in to the Secretary before the tickets are to be
signed by the Master and Secretary. It was recommended to the Secretary that he should acquaint
the members for to meet at 12 o'clock on St John's
day, and that the Stewarts should provide a proper
entertainment for that day. But as to the ball,
further than as above noticed, they recommend to the
Right Worshipfull and such of the members as are
in town for to meet any day they may think convenient, twixt this and St John's day, for to concert
what further may occur their anent."

March 25. "The Lodge having met as usuall, the 1772
Right Worshipfull reported that a committee of the
Lodge . . . had agreed for the purchase of an
area for the purpose of building a Lodge, at the price
of two hundred pounds sterg., which purchase the
members present give their assent." (The minute is
signed by all the members present except the committee.)

1772   May 5. The minutes and some copies of correspondence preserved now show the anxiety of the
Brethren to erect a proper Lodge and Inn in Inverness. Of this date the Master lays before the meeting a minute of agreement, dated 26th March 1772,
between him, as representing the Lodge, and Captain
John Grigor, as representing the Old Kilwinning
Lodge, on the one part, and Wm. Mackintosh, Esq.
of Holme.

September 15. The next meeting recorded in the
minutes took place on this date. It was convened by
the Master's order, in. order that the payment of the
subscriptions for the Lodges should commence. The
amount collected was £32. 11s.

November 30. "The Lodge having taken into
consideration the *progress* offered them by William
Mackintosh of Holm to the area on the East Street,
on which it was intended the Lodge should be built,"
a committee of six members was nominated, "and
any other member that chooses to attend, to consider
of the same in concert with the Sister Lodge."

December 28. From the minutes of this meeting
it appears as if the titles submitted by Holm were
not satisfactory, or from some other cause the ne-
gotiation with him apparently came to an abrupt
termination, for without any previous intimation we
read—"The Right Worshipful, with consent of the
Lodge, appoints the Wardens, Treasurer, and Secretary of the Lodge to meet with Andrew Tolmie for the
purchase of his house at Bridge Street, and in case of
failure to treat with any other person or persons for
the purchase of an area to build upon."

The building here referred to was long known as
Castle Tolmie, was situated at the foot of Bridge

Street, was latterly occupied as an inn, and was de- 1772
molished on the erection of the Suspension Bridge.

The Lodge (23 members present) made a charitable
collection at this meeting, and realised £1. 12s. 6d.,
equal to 1s. 6d. each.

A voucher for a purchase for this meeting is preserved among the loose papers, viz.:—

"December 28. For a Song Book, £0. 2s. 0d."

March 25. "The Right Worshipful made a pro- 1773
posal in presence of Captain John Grigor, Master ot
our Sister Lodge, of remitting the funds and subscriptions of the Lodge to Edinburgh, to be lodged in the
hands of a banker at interest, which was unanimously
approved of," and a committee was appointed to meet
with a committee of the Sister Lodge on 1st April.

March 31. A meeting of the committee appointed
to examine the Treasurer's accounts was held, when
the funds of the Lodge were found to be £50. 6s. 7d.
The Treasurer gave in a state of the subscriptions
received by him. "The committee find the amount
£124. 15s. *to be very right.*"

April 1. A meeting of the joint committee of
both Lodges took place in order to consider the state
of their funds. The funds of the Old Kilwinning
Lodge were found to be " £110. 15s. 7½d., exclusive
of their seventh share of the Trades House, of which
sum their cash at present in hand was £84. 14s. 10½d.,
which was paid in to the hands of Bailie John Mackintosh, Treasurer to the St Andrew Kilwinning
Lodge, who has of the funds of his Lodge £50. 6s. 7d.,
and of subscriptions collected, £124. 15s., which
three sums, amounting to £259. 16s. 5½d., the committee have ordered the Treasurer to remit Messrs
Mansfield, Hunter, & Co., bankers in Edinburgh, to

1773 be lodged in their hands, at 4 per cent. interest. The
said Treasurer is ordered to settle the sum of £260
neat, and to procure the said Bankers' note for the
same, payable at one day's date to the order of James
Baillie, Esq."

May 29. The Lodge resolve to wait on His
Excellency Lieut.-General Oughton, and, in concert
with the Sister Lodge, "an entertainment be given in
the Town Hall on Monday evening next."

May 31. The Lodges accordingly met, and waited
on His Excellency Lieut.-General Oughton. "Thereafter His Excellency did the Lodge the honour of
his presence at the Town Hall, where an entertainment was provided for the purpose, at the joint
expense of both Lodges."

1774 Nov. 30. "The Right Worshipful proposed that
the Treasurer writes Messrs Mansfield, Hunter, and
Co., to have their acceptance of £260 renewed, and
the interest included since the 23d April 1773, which
was unanimously approved of."

Dec. 27. It was resolved, "as a ball is generally
given the ladys on St John's day, that it should
hereafter be on St Andrew's day, as it is not so convenient for the Brethren in the country to attend on
St John's day; and that a committee should meet
some days prior to St Andrew's day, and resolve
whether a ball is to be given or not."

1775 February 23. After an interval of two and a-half
years, the Lodges make another effort to obtain a
site for their proposed building. At this meeting it
was resolved—"That as there are several areas in
town to be sold by the Magistrates, on Wednesday
the 1st March next, that a committee should meet
on Tuesday previous, in concert with a committee of

our Sister Lodge, to purchase any one area they shall think most proper for a building upon; at the same time, the committee resolve what length they are to go as to the price of such area before the auction."

March 25. "The committee reported to the meeting that they made purchase of an area on the west side of the Church Street, consisting of two roods, the purchase price being £50 sterling. The Lodge, taking into consideration that the ground is rather confined for their purpose, the Right Worshipfull, and Captain John Grigor of our Sister Lodge, at the request of the committee, were desired to bargain with the proprietor of the rood adjoining to the south, which they have done, the purchase price being £52. 10s. sterling.

"Thereafter there was a plan of the Lodge laid before the meeting, when they referred the same to the committee, with full powers to them to call in the subscriptions and receive estimates for putting the said plan in execution as they shall think most proper so to do."

November 30. The committee appointed some years ago to act with the committee of our Sister Lodge for carrying on the building of the intended Lodge, was reinforced by two new members, and empowered, "in conjunction with the committee of our Sister Lodge, to call in imediatly the subscriptions . . . not paid, and appoint two of their number . . . to take the superintendency of the said work, and do every other thing necessary their anent."

March 25. "This day being appointed for laying the foundation-stone of the New Lodge, it was proposed and agreed to that, in conjunction with our

1776 Sister Lodge, there should be a procession of both Lodges on that occasion, which, after turning the Lodge to a repast, was accordingly proceeded to."

November 29. " It having been suggested to the Lodge that no step had hitherto been taken for bringing to a sale a subject belonging to the Sister Lodge, they hereby instruct their committee formerly appointed to manage the affairs of the New Lodge, to apply to the Sister Lodge for having that subject brought to a public sale immediately, and in case they doe not comply with this request, it is the unanimous desire of this Lodge to their committee to break off all connections with the Sister Lodge, so far as regards the intended building, looking on such denial, if made, to be a conduct unworthy the connection this Lodge would wish to maintain with the Sister Lodge. In testimony of their unanimous approbation, this minutes is not only signed by the Master, but by the Officers and other Members present."

The price of aprons in 1776, compared with those in the present day, may be seen from the subjoined account :—

" The Santandrew of Inverness
                " To Willm. ffraser Glover.

	£	s.	d.
1776. To 2 doz. approns, at 12s. per doz.	£1	4	0
March 25. To cleaning 14, at 3d. each .	0	3	6
	£1	7	6
Received 20 old, at 3d. each .	0	5	0
	£1	2	6

February 7. The Lodges having found them- 1777
selves unable to carry on the new building, had
applied to Bailie John Mackintosh and Mr William
Cumming, two of their number, requesting that they
would take the whole charge upon themselves, and
in order that they might run no risk to their own
property, offered them full powers to collect subscriptions and borrow money on the subject itself, and
that the subject should be made over to them in
property, to remain in trust until they are relieved
from their engagements. To this proposal Bailie
Mackintosh and Wm. Cumming, "from an earnest
desire to promote anything so beneficial to the town
and country, had agreed." Of the steps taken, the
meeting highly approved, and "to facilitate the good
intentions of these gentlemen," unanimously came to
the following resolutions :—

" 1. The charters for the two areas purchased by
the Lodges to be made out in their names ;

" 2. That they shall have power of sale at any
time, upon three months notice to the Lodges ;

" 3. That a back bond be taken from them for
reconveying the subject to the Lodges upon being
reimbursed their outlays, and for paying to the
Lodges any balance remaining, in the event of their
being obliged to bring the subject to a sale ; and

" 4. That the thanks of the Lodge is justly due
to Baillie John Mackintosh and Mr William Cumming, for having so readily come in to a measure
upon which the success of the place of building
entirely depended."

May 12. Baillie John Mackintosh resigned his
office of Treasurer, "on account of being both

1777 Treasurer and Director of the intended building. The Lodge . . . return him their unanimous thanks for . . . a nine years faithful service." The Treasurer presented a state of his intromissions with the funds of the two Lodges, which was ordered to be engrossed in the minutes. By this account, it appears that the "plans" of the new building were prepared by John Fraser and Thomas Ross who were paid £3.

November 30. " The Lodge having been opened 1778 by Alexr. Baillie, Esq., last Past Master, our late Master, Captain Fraser of Culduthell, having de- ·parted this life since our last meeting (December 27), an event which the members sincerely regret."

Brother John Mackintosh reported that in order to carry on the new Lodge, he and Mr William Cumming had borrowed from Thomas Mackenzie of Ord, Esq., £200, and had their bond to the wife of Alexander Beaton, in Lochletter, for £60, for pay- ment of part of the area on which the Lodge is built. The meeting direct their Treasurer to pay the annual interest of these two sums as they become due.

A correspondence with the Right Honourable Lord Gardenstone is referred to in the minutes, but the subject is not mentioned, but is referred to in a petition addressed to the Commissioners of the Board of Annexed Estates, which is engrossed in the minutes, and is as follows:—

" The Representation of the Managers for Building a new Inn in the Town of Inverness:

" Sheweth,—That the Board was pleased in the month of March last to grant £200 as a help to carry on the said inn, and to promise £100 more in case a favorable report of the said was made by Sir Adolphus Oughton after having seen it:

"That the Managers find themselves very much in want of the additional help the Board was pleased to intend for them, and as Sir Adolphus Oughton did not come north this year, they beg leave to refer the Board to Lords Kaims, Gardenstone, and Anker-ville, and Major-General Skene, who have seen the progress made in the building:

"That the Managers expect the house and stables will be finished so as to receive a tenant at Martin-mas 1779, and as their only view in contributing so largely to this undertaking, and in the trouble they have necessarily had with it from the beginning, was that the publick, and especially the gentlemen who come to this country in publick capacities, shou'd be comfortably accommodated, and as the choice of a landlord is of the most material consequence towards making such accommodation complete; and as the Managers are desirous of shewing every mark of re-spect to patrons who have sssisted them so liberally; they unanimously beg leave to give the choice of a landlord for the said new inn to the Honourable Board, to the Lords of Justiciary, and to the Com-mander-in-Chief, and second in command in Scotland, and whoever is recommended by them shall receive the countenance and support of the Managers:

"Mr Charles Mackintosh will inform the Hon-ourable Board of any other particulars they wish to know, and will lay before them, if necessary, a list of candidates for the said inn."

The Treasurer's accounts for the years 1777-78, exhibited a subscription from Sir Eyre Coote of £50.

1779   November 30. The new Lodge is expected to be
Appoint-   finished against next Whitsunday, and it was "there-
ment of   fore now time to fix upon a landlord to occupy that
first
Tenant.   house.   They are of opinion that John Ettles, vintner
here, is the most proper person of all the candidates
for that station, being, from his behaviour hitherto
in that character, not only agreeable to them and
the publick, but also (as they are informed) the most
equal to the undertaking in point of capital."   The
Sister Lodge concurred in the choice of John Ettles
for landlord of the new Lodge and inn.   Thereafter a
committee was appointed, to meet on 8th December,
to fix on a yearly rent, and to treat with John Ettles
thereanent, "that he may be able to make every
preparation for entering and possessing the house in
quality of landlord against the said next term of
Whitsunday."

"The members present (there were only four)
were greatly chagrined at the neglect of so many of
their brethren to attend this meeting, and in particular as Brother Reid was in town, and did not
send a sufficient appology for his absence, the Lodge
determined to fine' him in five shillings, to be apply'd
towards the expense of the Lodge upon St John's
day next."

1780   June 3. Fifteen shillings ordered to be given to
the workmen employed in building and finishing the
new Lodge.

This was apparently the date of completion of the
new Lodge.   The contract for mason work was entered
into 26th June 1776.   John Ettles, the first tenant,
entered into possession Whitsunday 1780.

Mr John Ettles, the first tenant, appears to have

entered upon his occupancy with spirit. He presents 1780
a petition to the Lodge in 1780 showing the necessity
of having a coffee-room, tap, and bar properly fitted
up; to have another stable built, and " a brew's;" and
offers to effect these improvements at his own expense
on receiving a seven years lease from Whitsunday
following, and the value of the works at the termination of the lease. There is no mention in the minutes
as to what was done with this spirited offer.

Nov. 12. The minutes of a meeting of a com- 1781
mittee of both Lodges appointed to examine and
settle the accounts of the different tradesmen employed in building the Lodge are engrossed, and are
possessed of considerable interest. Collating several
other payments scattered through the accounts that
are engrossed, we find the cost of the building apparently as follows:—

Masonwork—Alexander Carmichael and Robert Duncan . , .	£801	0	6
Wright work—Colin Spence (deceased)	197	17	9½
Do., David Munro	15	0	0
Plaster work—Alexander Young .	141	12	4
Smith's work—James Fraser and William Wilson	14	0	0
Wood—Charles Cumming . .	4	3	0
Wood and Iron—Mackintosh, Shaw, and Co.	169	1	2
Glasier—Alexander Maclean (bal.) .	10	3	9
Nails, Hinges, Locks, &c.—Macpherson, Welsh, & Co. . . .	46	19	5
Carry forward . . £1399	17	11½	

1781	Brought forward . . £1399	17	11½
Nails, Hinges, Locks, &c.—To sundry tradesmen	21	11	7
" And Mr John Baillie, a sworn measurer, having been employed to measure the whole work, has given in a charge of £9. 2s. for his trouble," which the committee debit themselves with one-half, and the other half was . . to be borne by the different tradesmen	4	11	0
William Fraser, Town-Clerk, his account to compleat the titles .	12	3	1½
Going over references to the new Lodge we find there was also due to Mary Beaton for part of the area	60	0	0
While previous payments had been made for " plans " . . .	3	0	0
Paid the Town for area purchased .	51	5	0
Slater work—sundry tradesmen .	31	10	9½
Measuring the mason work . .	1	4	0
Sundry tradesmen . . .	33	1	10

£1618 5 3

The above estimate of the payments has been prepared with no little trouble, and probably does not show the total expenses of the building, as the whole of the payments to account to certain of the tradesmen cannot be found in the accounts preserved. There is, therefore, a probability that other items may have been paid, and that the whole cost of the building was about £1800.

In the same minute there appears a balance of 1781
£453 due to different tradesmen, while there were
mortgages on the building to the extent of £490,
showing the debt of the Lodges to amount to £943
—about half the probable cost of the Lodge.

Nov. 30. The Lodge approves of the Trustees
borrowing £250 from Captain John Mackintosh, of
the 73d Regiment, and empower them to grant an
heritable bond on the house.

August 12. A meeting of the committee of the 1782
two Lodges took place on this date. Bailie James
Shaw submitted his accounts, by which it appeared
there was a balance of £29. 14s. 6d. in his favour.

"The committee having carefully examined the
account, with the different vouchers, find the same
perfectly right, and do in name of the Lodges return
thanks to Mr Shaw for the *exact manner* in which
they have been kept."

The committee find their immediate liabilities
amount to £115, and after various proposals, resolve
to raise a sum of £400 by way of annuities, "as the
most probable chance of relieving the Lodges in time
of the debts they are at present burthened with."

Nov. 30. "The Right Worshipfull reported that
he and Mr William Cumming, of the Sister Lodge,
in whom the trust of the new Inn or Mason Lodge is
vested by both Lodges, had agreed with, and exchanged letters of lease with, John Ettles, innkeeper,
for the term of three years from Whitsunday next."
As the first lease of the new Lodge this document is
of some interest, and is here given :—

1782   " Sir,—We, as heritable proprietors in trust for the Mason Lodges of Inverness, of that large tenement lying on the west side of the Church Street of Inverness, commonly called by the name of the new inn or Mason Lodge, do hereby agree to let you in tack or lease for the space of three years from and after the term of Whitsunday next 1783, the foresaid tenement, with stables, coach-house, and whole pertinents thereto belonging, at the yearly rent of £50 sterling. . . . .

"As you propose, for your own further accommodation, building an additional stable along the river side at the foot of your closs, at your own proper expense, We hereby bind and oblige ourselves, on account of the Lodges, that you shall be allowed melioration for the same to the extent of £40 sterling, if it shall be found worth so much, or at whatever it shall be valued at not exceeding that sum by tradesmen mutually chosen by both parties, and this comprizement to be made and the value paid to you at the term of your removal from the subjects now lett to you.

" And as these subjects have been built by the Lodges, and by liberal subscriptions from individuals, for the sole purpose of the publick being well served in a good inn or tavern, as well as for the convenient accommodation of the members of the Lodges when they should have occasion to meet, it is hereby expressly provided and declared that you shall be obliged to keep the said house and pertinents in a proper manner, that you keep proper servants, and that the rooms shall be kept clean and in good order, so that travellers and the publick who go to your house shall have no just cause of complaint on ac-

count of bad service or bad usage. It being also 1782
hereby provided and declared that you shall at all
times be oblig'd to accommodate the members of both
Lodges when they have occasion to meet at your
house, or for the purpose of giving balls, or any other
purpose they may desire, with such of your best
rooms as they may want, in preference to every other
company.

   "We are, sir,
    "Your most humle. servts.,
      (Signed) "JOHN MACKINTOSH.
      (Signed) "WILLM. CUMING.
"To Mr John Ettles, vintner in Inverness.
 "Inverness, 22d Novemr. 1782."

Mr Ettles accepted this lease, and the Lodges
offered to accept payment of rent yearly at Whitsunday, instead of half-yearly, "in case it is more
convenient and agreeable to pay it in that way."

December 27. A committee appointed to act with 1784
a committee of the Sister Lodge, to "take under
their consideration the present state of the funds
and debts of the Lodges, and fix a plan for paying off
any balances due to tradesmen, and putting their
affairs on the clearest and most respectable footing in
their power."

February 5. The debts due by the Lodges 1785
amounted to £730 sterling, exclusive of an annuity
of £9 to Elizabeth Maccallum in return for £100
sunk by her. The interest of which sum of £730,
added to the annuity and the premium of insurance,
amount to an annual burthen of £48. 10s., leaving
of the present rent of £50 "an excrescence of £1

1785 10s. per annum. From this view of the situation of the affairs of the Lodges, it is plain that some plan must be fallen upon to lessen the heavy load of debt they are burthened with, otherwise the house must soon fall out of their hands." The committee resolve on energetic measures to get out of their difficulties. "It has occurred to the committee that the most probable means of effecting that desirable object will be the granting annuities for any sum or sums not exceeding £300." They accordingly resolve on measures likely to accomplish their object, and appoint trustees to receive proposals and fix the rates per annum with the different annuitants. "In order to establish a fund for paying the annuitants, the committee resolve that from and after next quarter day the quarter pennies of each Lodge shall be doubled"—that is, the members of the Old Lodge were each to pay 1s. per quarter, which, with admission dues or other sums, was to be paid once a-year to the Joint Treasurer; and the members of the new Lodge were to pay 2s. per quarter. The Old Lodge having a balance of £10. 10s., was directed to pay it into the hands of the Joint Treasurer.

The next step was an appeal to the burgh for assistance. "The committee, considering that no assistance has been yet given to the Lodges by the Town Counsal, although it must be acknowledged that the publick at large, and this place in particular, has been greatly benefited by the house erected by the Lodges for an Inn, and well knowing that all the members in Counsal will be inclined to give chearfully what aid can be afforded consistently with the attention they owe to the situation of the town's revenue, they do recommend it to the brethren who

are members of Counsal to make an application in 1785
name of the Lodges next Counsal day." Lastly, Mr
Wm. Cuming was desired to draw up an advertisement, for insertion in the different Edinburgh newspapers, for letting the house after the term of Whitsunday 1876, for such term of years as may be
agreed on, "the committee taking it into their serious
consideration how much it is their duty to make
every effort in their power for augmenting the rent
of the inn, and having it supply'd with a landlord
able to furnish it properly, and to give the public
satisfaction by his conduct."

March 25.—"Thereafter it was recommended to 1786
the Treasurer to write his correspondent at London
for different patterns of paper hangings in order that
a choice may be made of papers sufficient to finish
the different rooms in the inn agreeable to the engagement with the incoming tenant.

The lease with the new tenant, George Beverley,
was directed to be inserted in the minute-book. It
is as follows :—

"It is contracted, agreed, and ended between
Messieurs John Mackintosh, merchant, in Inverness,
and William Cuming, glazier there, as proprietors
and standing infeft in the subjects after-mentioned,
in trust for behoof of the members of the two different
Lodges of Masons in Inverness, on the one part; and
George Beverley, vintner at Fort-Augustus, as
princepall, and with and for him Duncan Macvicar,
barrack-master at Fort-George, and Lieutenant Alex-

1786 ander Fraser, at Bunchagovie, his cautioners, to the effect after-mentioned, on the other part; in manner following, viz., that is to say, the said John Mackintosh and William Cuming, with consent and approbation of a committee of said Lodges, have sett, and for the yearly rent under written, hereby sett, and in tack and assedation sett to the said George Beverley and his heirs (secluding assignees and subtenants, voluntary and legal) all and whole that new house in the Church Street of Inverness, commonly called the Mason Lodge, with the brewhouse, cellars, stables, byers, lofts, and others, with the pertinents, as the same are presently occupied by John Ettles, vintner in Inverness, and that for the space of ten full and complete years, from and after the term of Whitsunday 1786, which is hereby declared to be the term of the said George Beverley's entry thereto; but under these conditions—that as the premises are sett for the purpose of keeping an inn or tavern, in case the said George Beverley shall not behave to the satisfaction of the public in general in that character, it shall be in the power of the standing committees of the said Lodges, on proof thereof to their satisfaction, to declare this present lease void and null, and remove the said George Beverley at any term they shall see cause; as also that it shall be optional to the members of said Lodges, or their standing committees for the time, to accept of a higher rent for the said subjects, and to the said George Beverley to quit the possession thereof at the expiry of the first seven years, on the premonition of twelve months before to be made by either party to the other, under which conditions the said John Mackintosh and

William Cuming bind and oblige themselves, their 1786
heirs, successors, and the members of the said Lodges,
to warrant this present tack, and the subjects hereby
lett to the said George Beverley, at all hands and
against all deadly as law will: For the which causes,
and on the other part, the said George Beverley as
principal, and the saids Duncan Macvicar and Lieutenant Alexander Fraser as cautioners, securities, and
full debtors for and with him, bind and oblige themselves conjunctly and severally, their heirs, executors,
and successors, to content and pay to the said John
Mackintosh and William Cuming, their heirs or
assignees, or to the Treasurer appointed by the said
Lodges for the time, for the use and behoof of the
said Lodges of Masons, the sum of sixty-five pounds
sterling of yearly rent, at two terms in the year,
Whitsunday and Martinmas, in equal proportions,
beginning the first term's payment at Martinmas
1786 for the half-year preceding, and so forth half-
yearly thereafter, and to pay all public burthens
affecting the said subjects during the currency of
this lease; as also that he, the said George Beverley,
shall furnish the said house in a proper and sufficient
manner for the accommodation of the public, and
that he shall keep a sufficient number of servants in
his family for the serving of those who frequent his
house, that he shall also have two good post-chaises,
with able horses and careful drivers, and that he shall
not occupy a farm of larger extent than forty acres,
so as to withdraw the attention of himself or his servants from the business of the inn; and it is also
agreed that, in case he shall incline for his own accommodation to build an additional stable along the

1786 river-side at the foot of the close, he shall have liberty
to do so at the sight and by the approbation of the
standing committees of both Lodges, and shall have
allowance for the same at his removal, to the extent
of forty pounds, only if it shall be worth that sum,
according to the appretiation of tradesmen to be mutually chosen by the parties; and lastly, both parties
bind and oblige themselves and their foresaids to
perform the premises *hinc inde* to each other, under
the penalty of fifty pounds sterling, to be paid by the
party failing to the party performing or willing to
perform by and attour performance; and they consent to the registration hereof in the books of Council
and Session or others competent, that letters of
horning on six days' charge, and all other execution necessary may pass hereupon in form as effiers
whereto both parties constitute

their procurators, &c., In witness whereof these
presents wrote on this and the two preceding pages
of stampt paper, by Thomas Gilzean, Comptroller of
the Customs at Inverness, together with another
duplicate hereof, as subscribed by the said parties,
as follows, viz.: By the saids John Mackintosh,
William Cuming, and George Beverley, at Inverness
the first day of June 1785 years, before these witnesses, Robert Campbell, sheriff-clerk of Inverness,
and the said Thomas Gilzean; by the said Duncan
M'Vicar, at Fort-George, the third day of June
and year foresaid, before these witnesses, Duncan
Urquhart and James M'Grugar, both resideing at
Fort-George; and by the said Lieutenant Alexander
Fraser, at Inverness, the twentieth day of July and
year foresaid, before these witnesses, James Reid,

senior, merchant, Inverness, and Hugh Fraser, mes-   1786
senger there.

(Signed)

"Robert Campbell, witness.   John Mackintosh.
  Thomas Gilzean, witness.   William Cuming.
  Duncan Urquhart, witness.   George Beverley.
  James M'Gregor, witness.   Duncan M'Vicar.
  James Reid, witness.   Alexr. Fraser.
  Hugh Fraser, witness."

June 14. The following appears to be a draft or
copy of an advertisement, of which the cost, as
follows, was 15s. 6d.:—

"MASON LODGE AND NEW INN,
"INVERNESS, 14th June 1786.

"The two Mason Lodges of Inverness having
met here this day, do, in justice to George Beverley,
who entered into possession of this inn at Whitsunday last, express their particular satisfaction at finding the same neatly and elegantly fitted up, and
proper persons employed for attending to the business of the inn, from which they flatter themselves
that Mr B. will deserve the countenance of the
publick.

"The Lodges claim some merit in having got
this inn built at a time when there was none in this
place fit for the accommodation of the publick. They
appropriated the funds of both Lodges, which were
considerable, and procured contributions from the late
Commissioners of Annexed Estates, and from many
noblemen and gentlemen, and borrowed on their own
security what was further necessary for compleating

1786   this building; and as their sole object was to accommodate the publick, they consider it as their duty
not to receive or continue any innkeeper longer than
his conduct shall afford general satisfaction. They
therefore rely with confidence that, as they have
acted from impartial and disinterested motives in
the settlement of Mr Beverley, that this inn will
meet with proper support from the publick."

October 4. At a meeting of the committee of
the Lodges, they recommend the Treasurer " to in-
sist for payment of the balance of rent due by Mr
Ettles preceding his removal."

Mr Ettles had made certain alterations in the
stables which the Committee did not consider improvements. They "also called Mr George Beverley,
and recommended to him to alter the position of the
hakes in the stable, by making the same less perpen-
dicular, and removing the broad bars put in the said
hakes by Mr Ettles, and putting in the original
hakes, which are still in the possession of the said
Mr Ettles; and if he refuses to deliver the same,
they recommend to the Treasurer to apply for them
in proper form." It would therefore appear as if the
termination of the lease with John Ettles had not
been an amicable one.

At the same meeting, the committee accepted of
a proposal by Mrs Livingstone for sinking £150
upon her own life and the life of her daughter
Katherine, and £50 on the life of her daughter
Elizabeth. In respect of the old age of Mrs Livingstone, they granted bonds of annuity to her and her

daughter Katherine, or the longest lived of them, 1786 for £9, and to her daughter Elizabeth £4. 10s. in like manner.

The accounts of the Mason Lodges with their Treasurer, from August 1782 to December 1785, are engrossed following the preceding minute. The following entries seem of interest :—

Oct. 24. To cash paid insurance to Michaelmas, and posts	£2	16	7*
Feb. 3. To cash paid for one doz. aprons	0	6	0
April 23. To cash paid two algerines	1	1	0
Jan. 26. To cash paid insurance to Michaelmas 1785, &c.	2	6	0*
June 2. To cash paid Mr Gilzean for extending tack to Beverley	1	16	6
Oct. 15. To cash paid prem. of insurance	2	5	0*
To cash paid advertising the Lodge	0	15	6

November 30. "Brother John Mackintosh having presented to the Lodge some dozens of best flint glasses, with ' ST ANDREW-INES' ingraved on each, the brethren return him their most hearty thanks for the present, and many other marks of his attention and respect to the Lodge."

" Thereafter the Right Worshipful observed to the brethren that the Hon. Brother Archd. Fraser of Lovat had offered to the Lodge a sett of benches, for the accommodation of the ladies in the Town Hall, and therefore moved that the said offer should

1786   be accepted, of which the Lodge agreed to do, and
returned their sincere thanks to Brother Fraser for
his genteel present, and desire that the same should
be recorded in these minutes."

1789   January 10. At a meeting of the committee of
both Lodges held this day, the state of the Lodge
funds was considered. The debts due by them were
£630. 12s., and the annuities amounted to £22. 10s.
After payment of the interest on the debts, the
annuities, and the insurance, there was a growing
fund of £8. 15s., exclusive of admissions and quarter
pennies, from which view of their affairs the committee resolved to receive another £100 on annuity.

"The committee thereafter, in virtue of the
powers given them by the Lodges, took under their
consideration an application made by George Beverley, their tenant, respecting that he had suffered
considerably since he had taken possession of the
inn by sickness, and other unfavourable circumstances, and praying, therefore, for such aid as the
Lodges might see proper to bestow on him; and the
committee being satisfied that Mr Beverley's representation is well-founded, they have resolved to
make him a present of £15 . . . and at the
same they intimate to Mr Beverley that this is not
to be considered as a precedent, and that no application of like nature will be attended to."

February 5. Poor Mr Beverley had no opportunity of quoting this liberality of the committee as
a precedent, as his death took place before their next
meeting on 5th February. On that date a letter
from Mr M'Vicar was read, praying to be released

from his engagement, as cautioner for the late Mr 1789
Beverley, for payment of the future rents of the inn
during the continuance of the lease.   The committee
refused his request, but resolve "most readily, as
societies or individuals, to give him every assistance
in their power to get a proper tenant for the house."
They draw up an advertisement to be transmitted to
Mr M'Vicar "that if he approves of it, he may send
it to Edinburgh to be inserted in the newspapers."

"To Let, and enter at such term as may be agreed
on, that large commodious Inn in Inverness, the property of the Mason Lodges there, and late in the
occupation of the deceast George Beverley.

"The House, which was built at a very great expense with the sole view of affording elegant accommodation to travellers, contains four dining parlours,
a large hall for public meetings, a number of elegant
bedrooms, two good kitchens, large cellars, larder,
servants' hall, landlady's bedroom, barr, &c., &c., with
capital stables and coach-house attached.

"The House is in full trade, and will be kept so
by Mrs Beverley till it is entered on by another person.

"The furniture is well chosen and in very good
order, having been purchased new from the very best
markets about two years past, and will be given to an
incoming tenant at a fair appropriation.

"Such as choose to give in proposals may transmit
them to Mrs Beverley at the Inn, or to Mr Duncan
M'Vicar, barrackmaster at Fort-George, to be by them
laid before the Lodges.

The committee resolve that although "they agree

13

1789 to Mr M'Vicar's advertising for a tenant, yet that
he shall not have the power of concluding a bargain
with any man until they are satisfied with his character and abilities, so as care may be taken that the
inn do not fall into improper hands."

August 22. "The Lodge having met to determine
on a procession at laying the foundation-stone of the
new Court-house steeple, and being joined by a committee of the Sister Lodge, they have resolved that
their procession shall be on the following plan:—

The Old Lodge to take precedence, and that the
Lodges shall each of them proceed in the same order
exactly, which is to be as under—

1. The Tyler with a drawn sword, uncovered.
2. The Bible carried by two operative masons, un-
    covered.
3. The Master.
4. The Past Masters, two and two.
5. The Wardens,   do.
6. The Treasurer and Secretary.
7. The Brethren, two and two, according to
    seniority.
8. The Stewards.
9. Two operative masons with drawn swords.
10. That all the brethren shall be dressed on that
    day in black coats, vest, and britches, with
    white stockings and gloves.

That both Lodges shall meet on the day of procession (which is fixed for Friday next, the 28th
curt.) at eleven o'clock in the forenoon, and that the
procession shall commence exactly at 12 o'clock.

That after the procession is ended, the Lodges

shall return to their respective Lodge Rooms, and 1789 dine and spend the evening together.

Owing to the death of their Treasurer, Robert Rose, the Lodges appoint John Falconer to be their Joint Treasurer.

August 28. "The brethren proceed to the procession agreeable to the minute of 22d inst. Previous thereto, a roll of vellum, with the following inscription, was sealed up in a bottle and deposited in the foundation-stone :—

"In the year of our Lord 1789, and the reign of King George the Third the twenty-ninth, the foundation of this steeple was laid in presence of Phineas Mackintosh, Esq., Provost of Inverness; Messrs Alexander Shaw, John Mackintosh, James Shaw, Robert Warrand, Baillies; and William Inglis, Dean of Guild; by the Right Worshipfull John M'Gregor, Master of the Old Inverness Kilwinning Lodge, and the Right Worshipfull William Inglis, Master of the New Inverness St Andrew Kilwinning Lodge, assisted by the Brethren of the

"*New Lodge.*—The Tyler with a drawn sword; the Bible, borne by two Master Masons; Mr Thomas Walcot, P.M.; Simon Fraser, Esq., P.M.; John Mackintosh, Esq., P.M.; James Fraser, Esq., S.W.; Æneas Mackintosh, Esq., J.W.; John Falconer, Esq., Treasurer; Charles Jamieson, Secretary; Mr William Scott; Mr James Shaw; Doctor James M'Leod; Alexander Fraser, Esq.; Mr Alpin Grant; Mr Thos. Gilzean; Mr James Robertson; Thomas Fraser, Esq. of Newtown; William Mackintosh, Esq.; Mr James Reid; Doctor William Kennedy, Stewart.

1789   "*Old Lodge.*—The Tyler with a drawn sword; the Bible and Cushion, borne by two Master Masons; Thomas Young, P.M.; William Cuming, P.M.; Robert Anderson, P.M.; Alex. M'Leod, S.W.; John Mackenzie, J.W.; James Reid, Treasurer; Thomas Monro, Secretary; Simon Fraser; James Blair; William Welsh; Capt. M'Kinnon; Campbell Mackintosh; Alex. Macdonald; John M'Gregor; Henry Andrews; Alex. Mackenzie; Hugh Fraser and James Macdonald, Stewarts.

"The foresaid stone being laid in due form amidst the acclamations of an immense crowd of the inhabitants and people from the country."

The expenses of the procession paid to Mrs Beverley amounted to £3. 18s. 10d.

1790   Jan. 6. At a committee of both Lodges, £1. 8s. 6d. allowed to Mrs Beverley for the cost of an illumination, as ordered by the Lodges in March last, on account of his Majestie's happy recovery.

Dec. 29. The Committee examined the state of debt, &c., due by the Lodges.—   .

The sums borrowed amounted to £650.

Interest thereon, at 5 per cent.	. £32	10	0
Annuities—Mrs M'Callum .	. 9	0	0
Do. Mrs Livingstone and her daughter	9	0	0
Do. Mrs M'Callum further .	. 4	10	0
Insurance prem. from fire .	. 2	5	0
Annual stent . . .	. 1	1	8
	£58	6	8

The Old Lodge appoint of their Lodge as the new

trustees, Mr Alex. Macleod, Baillie Thomas Young, 1793
and Mr Campbell Mackintosh; the New Lodge,
Baillie William Inglis, Simon Fraser of Farraline,
and Mr James Grant.   "Both Lodges agree that
they be invested with the said property as trustees
for both Lodges, and they remit to the said Simon
Fraser; Thomas Gilzean, Sheriff-Substitute of Inverness-shire; the said James Grant, and Mr Campbell
Mackintosh, to cause and make out the necessary
writing for carrying this plan to effect."

The strange curtness of this minute, without any
reference to the services of Bailie John Mackintosh
and Wm. Cuming, after a period of nearly seventeen
years as trustees of the new inn (having been appointed 7th February 1777), will be noticed.   They
had accepted the responsibility of the debts, &c., of
the Lodges when there was danger and difficulty in
doing so, and as appears by the minutes, had laboured
zealously and successfully in their behalf, yet are now
simply dismissed without a word of thanks!

November 30. "It having been determined at a 1794
former meeting not to continue John Hay as tenant
to the Lodge after Whitsunday 1795, the brethren
present think it necessary that the standing committee of both Lodges shall meet upon the 2d Dec. to
consider respecting the mode of letting the house, &c.,"
which resolution was approved of by the sister Lodge.

Dec. 29. The committee of both Lodges find the
accounts of William Wilson, their Joint Treasurer,
"fairly stated and properly vouched."

May 1. The committee (of the two Lodges) met 1795
in order to take into consideration the proposal made

1795 by William Fraser, vintner in Inverness, to become their tenant for the Lodge, and considering the general good character of the man, and that he is honest and sober, they very readily agree to let him have it for a year from Whitsunday first on trial, three months' premonition to be given by the Lodges or by him if either party chuse to be off at the end of the year. And although the committee did not think it would be prudent to make any diminution of the rent presently paid for the house, yet they promised Mr Fraser that an allowance would be made to him for the disadvantage he might be put to by removing from his own house so near to the term, and some other inconveniences which his entering into the Lodge at so short notice has subjected him to.

Aug. 18. At a meeting of the trustees for both Lodges they accepted a loan of £400 from Thomas Warrand, Esq. of Newton, and to grant him an heritable bond over the Lodge in security, the money to be applied in discharging the bond due to the heirs of Captain John Mackintosh for £250, bill to Alex. Fraser, £100, and a bill for £50 discounted on account of the Lodge.

1796 Dec. 29. The joint committee fixed the rent of the Lodge to be paid by William Fraser at £45 per annum.

"The committee, wishing to take proper care of the interest of the Lodge, and also to give reasonable encouragement to their tenant, Wm. Fraser, while he continues to behave as he has hitherto done, have agreed with him that from Whitsunday next the rent shall be £50 per annum, at which sum they have agreed it shall continue untill the Lodges or their

committee shall otherways determine." If the rent 1796
was to be raised the tenant was to get notice on St
John's preceding the Whitsunday at which such rise
was to take place.

1796   EXTRACT OF ACCOUNTS.
Jan. 18. Paid John Mackenzie, glover, for
                24 new aprons   .   .   £1   4   0
Dec. 24. Paid Farraline, per receipt, being
                what he paid for advertisements
                in the newspapers for the Mason
1797   Lodge 4 10   6
July 6. By cash received from M'Intosh,
                Scott, Inglis, Shaw, & Co. for
                13½ stone iron, being what was
                on the old sign of the Lodge, at
                2s.   1   7   0
Nov. 30. By cash received for old leather
                aprons sold to Dr Robertson . 0 8 0

November 30. "The Secretary was desired to 1797
order a copy of the late publication on Masonry by
Mr Sommers, Clerk of the Grand Lodge, under the
sanction of the Lodge, and to deposit that copy in
the chest for the use of this Lodge."

A meeting of the committee of the two Lodges
in Inverness (Old Lodge and New Lodge), together
with the Master of the Clachnacuddin Operative
Lodge, met on 6th December, " being the committee
appointed for conducting the intended procession on
St John's day, and resolved that at twelve o'clock
on that day the *two* Lodges shall assemble in the
Northern Meeting Rooms. That the procession

1797   shall take place precisely at one o'clock thro' the different streets in town, and return to the Mason Lodge. . . . That in the procession the senior Lodge shall take precedence, as has been usual in this place, and that such members of the Clachnacuddin Operative Lodge as incline to join the procession shall fall into the rear. . . . That the dress of the day shall be black, with white stockings and aprons, without ornaments. The Treasurers are requested to direct that the rods, rules, and battens of both Lodges be in proper order; the cusheons, squeres, &c., brushed up, if necessary."

December 27. Saint John's day (20 members present). The brethren having assembled in the Northern Meeting Rooms, they walked in procession to church, preceded by the Old Sister Lodge, and followed by the New Clachnacuddin Lodge, both of this place. The Rev. Mr Alexander Fraser, one of the ministers of this place, preached an excellent sermon to the three Lodges, from the first verse of the 133d Psalm as his text, which sermon was unanimously approved of by the brethren. After sermon the three Lodges walked in procession through the different streets of Inverness, and then the brethren of this Lodge went to the Mason Lodge. The meeting closed at *eight* o'clock.

As appears by an entry in their accounts of 28th December, the Lodges were led in the procession by the band of the Hopetown Fencibles, for whose services they paid £6. 6s.

Dec. 31. Committee of both Lodges having taken into consideration the state of the affairs of the Lodges, they find that the Lodges are due to

Thomas Warrand, Esq. of Lentran	£400	0	0	1798
Mrs Mackintosh of Dochgerrach	200	0	0	
Misses Maclean . . .	100	0	0	
	£700	0	0	

And the following liferent annuities :—

Mrs Macallum, Inverness . .	£9	0	0
Mrs Grant of Tullochgorum .	15	0	0
Mrs Livingstone, at Inverness .	13	10	0
	£37	10	0

The committee further considering that the house
and office-houses belonging to the Lodges were let to
William Fraser at the low rent of £50, as an encouragement for him to take them at the time ; but
that since Mr Fraser's entry he has got himself very
well established in business, and is now in a condition to pay an adequate rent. The committee are
therefore of opinion that after Whitsunday 1800 Mr
Fraser ought to pay £60 sterling of yearly rent for
the Lodge, and that notice should be given him at
next Saint Andrew's day.

Among the items in the accounts are :—

1797

Jan. 10. To paid assessment for levying men for the army and navy	£1	1	7½
April 5. To paid stent	0	13	4
Dec. 28. To paid the Band of the Hope- 1798 town Fencibles . . .	6	6	0
Jan. 10. To paid Geo. Urquhart for a new cusheon, square, and compass .	3	7	1
To paid Mr Davidson for a new book	0	6	6

1799   There is no minute recording the proceedings at
the laying of the foundation-stone of the Infirmary;
but the following items appear in the Joint Treasurer's accounts :—

May 15. To paid two pairs white gloves for
            Tylers at the procession laying
            foundation of the Infirmary £0 4 0
            To paid the band .   . . 2 4 0
            To paid parchment for inscription 0 4 6
            To cash laid under the foundation-
            stone, and coins .   . . 1 2 0
            To cash to guard for keeping off
            the mob 1 11 6

A full account, however, of the laying of the foundation-stone has been given from the minutes of the
St John's Old Lodge.

Nov. 30. A communication was received from
the Grand Lodge intimating that they proposed to
erect at Edinburgh a Free Masons' Hall, " with
proper accommodation for the brethren of Scotland,
which would be highly convenient and creditable to
the craft, of real advantage to the institution, and
honourable to the metropolis." The Master reported
that he had replied " expressing the wishes of the
Lodge for the success of the undertaking, but that
the present state of the funds could not admit of
their giving any aid, but that before the work was
far advanced some aid would be given by the individual members of this Lodge," which answer was
unanimously approved of.

The Master reported that in compliance with the
Act passed in the last session of Parliament, cap. 79,
entitled " An Act for the more effectual suppression

of societies established for seditious and treasonable 1799
purposes, &c.," he had caused record with the Clerk
of the Peace a signed list of the attending members of
this Lodge, duly sworn to by him and the Secretary,
as required by law, and of which he now presented
an extract, which was read and approved of.

Dec. 28. Committee of both Lodges. Conference
with William Fraser, their tenant. Lease to be
granted for nine years, commencing at Whitsunday
1800, but optional to him and the Lodge to be free at
the end of every three years upon six months notice.
Rent £60.

The Right Worshipful the Master of the Old 1800
Sister Lodge represented that he was credibly informed that the Inverness Clachnacuddin Operative
Sister Lodge had in a late instance granted a dispensation to certain of its members, who, in consequence thereof, have taken upon themselves to hold
a Mason Lodge in Badenoch, and on that occasion to
admit Master Masons as well as entered Apprentices;
and what is now represented having been confirmed
by a brother who attended the Lodge held in
Badenoch as above, the committee are of opinion
that the granting such deputations, and holding
Lodges and admitting Masons in consequence thereof,
is not only contrary to the rules of Masonry, but
likewise to the tenor of the late Act of Parliament
granting certain privileges to Lodges properly constituted; and as the said Operative Lodge obtained
their charter on the recommendation of these Lodges,
they considered it their duty to watch over her conduct, and to guard her against committing such irregularities. With that view a message was sent by

1800 the proper officer to the office-bearers of said Lodge,
requesting their attendance, in order to explain and
account for their conduct. But having understood
that the Right Worshipful was from home, and the
other office-bearers having declined to appear, the
committee, before taking further measures in this
affair, agreed to meet on Monday next, the fifth of
January, and directed that notice of such meeting
should be given by the Tyler to the office-bearers of
the said sister Lodge, and their attendance be again
required on that day.

1801   Jan. 5. The Right Worshipful the Master and
office-bearers of the Inverness Clachnacuddin Operative Lodge having attended, in consequence of the
message from these Lodges, and having been questioned on what is stated in the minutes of the 31st
ult., they acknowledged having granted a deputation
for holding a Lodge in Badenoch, and, in excuse,
pleaded that a similar practice prevailed in several
other Lodges in the North, and that they were not
aware that the doing so was either improper or contrary to the established rules of Freemasonry. They
were warned of the illegality and irregularity of their
conduct in this particular; and they severally engaged to communicate this to the first meeting of
their Lodge, to recall immediately the deputation, to
avoid the like practice in future, and to report the
measures adopted in their Lodge in consequence of
the present conference.

1803   December 27. A committee appointed to meet a
committee of the sister Lodge to consider of the
most eligible measures to adopt for borrowing money
to discharge the debt of £400 originally due to Mr

Warrand of Lentran, and now conveyed to Mr 1803
Fraser of Farraline, and for the payment whereof, a
demand has been made by Farraline on the Lodge.
Also, to consider of an application and proposal by
*_James_ Fraser, their tenant, for some additions to the
present buildings, necessary for a barr, and for his
accommodation.

There was laid before the Lodge a letter from 1804
the Secretary of the Grand Lodge of Scotland, 29th
October 1804, stating "that a society of persons of
some respectability in life, in a town not many miles
distant from Edinr., have possessed themselves of certain pamphlets pretending to lay open the secrets of
our order, and in consequence thereof, have not only
held mock Lodges, but have taken bets that they
will gain admittance into regular Lodges. Although
from any information to be obtained from these
ridiculous publications, we know that nothing is to
be apprehended, yet in order to prevent all and every
visiting stranger who has not been regularly entered a mason, from obtaining admission into an
open Lodge, the Grand Lodge recommend," besides
examining such stranger, to administer an oath, according to form subjoined, to be subscribed by the
stranger, in presence of two or more office-bearers,
"who will also subscribe along with him as witnesses.
This, it is believed, will deter even the most profli-

---

* As appears by a notice in the papers last year (1876)—
" Mr William Fraser, vintner, Mason's Lodge (now Caledonian Hotel), Inverness, died there in 1802." His son
James, who succeeded him as tenant, emigrated to America,
and died at Wellsville, Ohio, on the 20th August 1874. He
must have lived to an extreme old age, having been tenant
of the Mason Lodge in Inverness 72 years previously.

1801 gate, as they must be aware of the consequence of a criminal prosecution for perjury." The Lodge resolved to adopt the plan recommended.

Dec. 1. The Lodge avail themselves of the optional breach, in favour of either party, in the lease between them and their tenant, James Fraser, "and being of opinion that the tenant can well afford to give some addition to the present rent," they arrange with him, after a conference, that the yearly rent will be £100 for the six years of his lease to run after Whitsunday, and that the optional breach in favour of the Lodge should be given up for these six years, and that the Lodge should build a proper place for a bar.

1805   August 16. The committee of both Lodges approved of a loan of £200 from Kenneth Mackenzie, farmer at Culduthel, for the expense of putting up a new bar and other repairs.

December 27. It was agreed that the Lodge should in future meet quarterly, at seven o'clock in the evening, on

Lady day ....25th March.
St John Baptist........................24th June.
St Michael's.............................29th Sept.
St John the Evan.....................27th Dec.
And on St Andrew's day ....30th Nov.

December 30. A committee of both Lodges— Mr Wilson stated that Miss Nancy Fraser, daughter of the late Captain Simon Fraser of Fanellan was willing to give the Lodges £200, on an annuity of £20 per annum, which they agreed to accept, and to pay up the loan of £200 borrowed from Kenneth Mackenzie at Culduthel.

June 10. Committee of both Lodges. In order 1807
to repay Mr Fraser of Farraline the sum of £300, it
was suggested that it would be necessary to borrow
that sum, and a proposal was made in name of Miss
Martha Mackintosh, daughter of the deceased Provost
William Mackintosh, for sinking the sum of £300 upon
an annuity of ten per centum per annum, during her
natural life, which proposal was agreed to by the
committee.

July. " A procession took place (along with the
other two Lodges in Inverness) when laying a foundation-stone of the bridge across the river Ness from
near the Old Quay to *the new village at Merkinch.*
The Honble. and Right Worshipful Master (Lovat)
presided on the occasion. The same form and order
followed as that at laying the foundation-stone of the
Royal Infirmary.

June 17. Committee of both Lodges. " It having 1808
been represented to the committee by Mr James
Fraser, the tenant of the house, that the lower part
thereof is in considerable disrepair, owing to the vast
quantity of rats that came in by the lower drains,
these apartments, notwithstanding of every exertion
made by him, is almost uninhabitable. That the
barr lately built is also in danger of being destroyed
by the great fall of water from the house, which fall
has also greatly injured the rest of the house." Mr
James Smith, architect, was ordered to give in an
estimate of the cost of the necessary repairs.

June 24. A letter received from the Secretary
of the Grand Lodge " relative to an unpleasant dispute 'twixt Mr Gilren and Dr Mitchell, of Edinburgh," was read, and the Master directed to convey

1808 to the Grand Lodge that this Lodge approved of their proceedings, and that the brethren "highly disapprove of the conduct of any brother which has a tendency to destroy that subordination to the Grand Lodge, and that harmony which has formerly distinguished the craft, and which appears to them so necessary for the support of the Grand Lodge, and the preservation of the ancient principles of Masonry."

1809 December 30. Committee meeting of both Lodges. Mr James Fraser, the tacksman of the Mason Lodge, having been asked "what his intentions were respecting his continuing as tenant after the expiry of his present lease at Whity. 1811," gave no satisfactory answer, but "declared explicitly that he would give no additional rent, and that the premises stood very much in need of repair," the committee resolved to advertise the Lodge for set at Whity. 1811, "three times in the 'Inverness Journal' at the distance of 14 days, and once in each of the three *provincial* Edinburgh newspapers ;" and they remit to a committee to fix the terms upon which the Lodge will be let.

1810 September 7. An offer, dated the 27th day of July last, by Mr Peter Anderson, writer, Inverness, in name of the Caledonian Company, for a lease of the Mason Lodge at £130 per annum of rent, was accepted upon the following conditions :—

"The lease to be for seven years from Whity. 1811, with a power of subset with the approbation of the trustees of the house ; the trustees to put

the house in a tenantable state of repair, and to put 1810
four storm windows instead of the present skylights
in the garrets ; the tenants to leave the premises in
the same state, fair wear and tear excepted ; and the
tenants to make improvements on the buildings to
the extent of £313. 8s. 6d., to be given over at
valuation at the end of the lease."

The lease was to be signed by Richard Gregory,
Esq.,* and Mr Anderson, for themselves and the re-
manent members of the Caledonian Company. The
lease was signed on 3d January 1811.

December 27. The election of a new Master takes
place, "in place of the late Worthy Farraline, whose
death the whole brethren deeply regret." He died
on 21st August 1810.

January 19. "The members of both Lodges are 1811
to dine together, with as many of *their respectable
friends* as chuse to attend, on Friday, 8th February
next, at 4 o'clock. The Masters of both Lodges, and
their office-bearers, are appointed, along with Provost
Grant and Dr Robertson, as a committee to arrange
matters for the dinner."

November 30. "An application from the Clach- 1812
nacuddin Lodge of Inverness, No. 259 of Scotland,
praying for an aid to help their new building in
Inverness to accommodate their brethren, was read
and ordered to be taken into consideration on next
St John's day."

December 28. "The Lodge being opened in due

* It was after this Mr Gregory or Gilbert, that Gilbert
Street, Merkinch, was named.

14

1812 form, proceeded to the election of a Master and office-bearers for the ensuing year, when the present worthy Right Worshipful Dr Robertson (who has for the last year, with much credit to himself and the greatest pleasure to the brethren, filled the office) was unanimously re-elected Master, and the Doctor having taken the chair, was accordingly congratulated and saluted Master for the ensuing year."

"Mr David Inglis was, upon due trial and examination, found to have been made a Fellow-craft, and raised to the sublime degree of Master Mason, in a well constituted Lodge at Bombay, and he was now received into his *Mother's* Lodge as an excellent and worthy brother returned from the East."

"The Tyler's salary increased to 30s. per annum.

"Thereafter a collection was made for the poor, as usual, when £10. 14s. 6d. sterling was collected, including five guineas from our worthy respectable Brother, Lovat, who never forgets his indigent brethren."

1813   January 6. Committee meeting. Insurance on Lodge ordered to be increased to £2000.

The Old Lodge having reported that they doubled their fees, the New Lodge resolved, with their consent, to make the fees in future as follows :—Entering, £2. 12s. 6d.; passing, £1. 1s.; raising, £1. 1s.

1814   January 3. Lovat continues his £5. 5s. subscription.

1815   January 7. Committee meeting. Farraline's bond of £100 directed to be paid off. There then remains of debt on the Lodge, bond to Miss McLean, of Dochgarroch, £100 ; and the following annuities:—

Mrs Grant of Tullochgorum	£15	0	0
Miss May Mackintosh .	20	0	0
Miss Martha Mackintosh .	30	0	0
Miss Ann Fraser, Fanellan	20	0	0

June 13. Committee meeting. Resolved that, in 1817 consideration of all the other public and corporate bodies in town and county having subscribed towards the funds for the support of the labouring poor, and that the county of Inverness has also subscribed very liberally to the purpose, and that the different individuals in town have also subscribed, this committee allot ten guineas towards the above laudable purpose.

January 3. Committee meeting. The committee 1818 having taken into their consideration that the lease of the Mason Lodge will expire at Whitsunday next, and that Mr William Bennet, the present tenant under the Caledonian Company, has made an offer for a five years' lease, on condition of getting certain additional buildings, for the expense of which he is willing to allow $7\frac{1}{2}$ per cent. interest, appoint a special committee to confer with Mr Bennet on the subject.

January 10. The committee agreed with Mr Wm. Bennet for a five years' lease from Whitsunday 1818, at a yearly rent of £110. "It is also stipulated that Mr Bennet is in future to give the same accommodation as at present to the passengers of the Caledonian Co. and of the mail coach during the currency of his lease, and Mr Bennet becomes bound not to enter into any speculation prejudicial to those establishments, which is also to be a condition of the lease."

January 20. "Mrs Grant of Tullochgorum, an 1820 annuitant, died in March last."

1820   A "view of what each Lodge contributed to the
common stock since the year 17—, when the house
called 'The Mason Lodge' was built," was ordered
to be engrossed in the minute book of the Lodge.
It is to be regretted that this was not done, as the
account would be of considerable interest.

It having been mentioned that there is a prospect
of Miss Munro's property behind the stables being
brought to sale in the course of this year, the Masters
of both Lodges are recommended to treat with the
seller, and to purchase the property, "if it can be
acquired on moderate terms."

1823   October 17. Mr Bennet intimates his intention of
giving up the house at Whitsunday 1824.   "But he
mentions his readiness to accommodate his successor,
providing he took the whole household furniture,
bed and table linen, the stock of wine and spirits,
the horses and chaises, &c., at a valuation, that is to
say, he would allow his successor either to enter a
month or two *before,* or a month or two *after* the
term."   The committee accepted Mr Bennet's re
signation, and directed advertisements to be inserted
in the Inverness papers, Aberdeen Journal, Perth
Courier, Edinburgh Courant and Journal, and the
Glasgow News, called the Chronicle, and to specify
in said advertisement what Mr Bennet proposes.

Dec. 1. Thirteen applications (from parties in
Edinburgh 5, Glasgow 2, and other towns) submitted.
The committee decided upon a five or seven years
lease, at £120, the tenant to uphold the whole property, and be at the expense of the interior decora-
tions, and the question of additional buildings for
bedrooms, &c., to be fixed by minute.   These terms

were explained to the two candidates who appeared 1823
before the committee, and the meeting adjourned till
22d current.

March 23. " It is now fixed that Mr Robert 1824
Wilson, of Paisley, is to be the new tenant of the
Lodge, &c., in the room of Mr Bennet, who leaves
the premises on or before the 26th May 1824."

March 30. A general meeting of the St John's
and St Andrew's Lodges of Inverness was held to-
day. There were 21 members present of the former
Lodge ; of St Andrew's, only 4—office-bearers. Extensive improvements and additions to the Lodge
were resolved upon, being new buildings to the rear
of the Lodge, and new stables and coach-house, &c.
Advertisement calling for tenders was ordered to be
inserted in the papers.

April 26. Committee meeting. The tender of Mr
James Smith, architect, for the new buildings, not
including the stables and coach-house, was accepted
for £1430, on his departing from any charge for
preparing the plans and specifications, and Mr Wilson,
the new tenant, agreed to pay 7 per cent. on the cost
of any additions made to the present accommodation.

The committee instructed the purchase of a piece
of ground adjoining the property of the Lodges, belonging to the heirs of the late Mr Peter Anderson,
at a price not exceeding £100. It was acquired for
£95.

June 1. Thomas Mackintosh, mason, Nairn, appointed overseer of the new works at £1. 1s. per
week.

The value of the improvements made by Mr
Bennet found to be £191. 3s. 8d.

1824   Miss May Mackintosh, one of the annuitants on the property, proposed to the Lodges to sell her annuity to them, which offer they declined.

August 16. Contract entered into with Messrs Thomas Macfarlane, mason, and Donald Macphail, carpenter, for building the new stables and coach-house for £639, from which sum they offer to deduct £80 if the stables and shed now on the stance shall be given to them : the payments were to be in three instalments, one-third *when the work commences*, one-third when roofed in, and one-third when taken off the contractors' hands.

1825   November 30. General meeting of both Lodges. Provost Grant and Mr Campbell Mackintosh, the two surviving trustees, stated that by the appointment of the general meeting of 30th March 1824, they had assumed Provost James Robertson of Inverness; Thomas Gilzean, Sheriff-Substitute of Inverness-shire; Affleck Fraser, Esquire of Culduthel; Bailie Robert Smith, merchant in Inverness; John Edwards, solicitor there, and John Ferguson, merchant there, as joint trustees along with themselves, in room of the former trustees who are now dead.

The trustees reported that, for enabling them to defray the expenses of the new building and improvements, they had obtained a cash credit from the Bank of Scotland on their own bond and a disposition of the property of the Lodges, on which the Bank had been infeft.

1826   Feb. 26. The committee come to an arrangement with Mr Wilson, their tenant, as to the rent he is to pay in future. The rent was thus fixed—

Rent of the old house £120   0   0   1826
Interest on £1500, the expense of the
    new buildings, at the rate of 7 per
    cent. on the outlay thereof .   .   105   0   0
                                        ————————————
        Total rent   .   .   . £225   0   0

commencing as from Whitsunday last, and to continue during his lease, and with which yearly rent
Mr Wilson declared himself satisfied.

April 11. The committee find that the state of
their funds will admit of their paying off Miss Mac-
lean's bond for £100, and give instructions accordingly.

————

The following extracts from the minutes were
omitted at page 196:—

Jan. 23. A meeting of the joint committee was   1792
held this day, when a letter from the cautioners of
the late Mr Beverley was read, requesting the Lodge
to advertise the inn, while they still remained bound
for the rent.   The Lodge accordingly drew up the
following advertisement, to be inserted in two of the
Edinburgh newspapers, and in the Aberdeen newspapers:—

    "To Lett, and enter on Whitsunday next,
    "That large and commodious Inn and Tavern at
Inverness, the property of the Mason Lodges there,
and now in the occupation of Mrs Beverley.   The
house, which was built at a very great expense, with

1792 the sole view of affording elegant accommodation to travellers, contains four dining parlours, a large hall for publick meetings, a number of elegant bedrooms, two good kitchens, large cellars, larder, servants' hall, landlady's bedroom, barr, &c., &c., with capital stables and coach-house attached.

"The house is in full trade, and will be kept so by Mrs Beverley till it is entered by another person.

"From the situation of this house, and the number of gentlemen who interest themselves in its success, there cannot be a doubt that any man who possesses it, and will exert himself to give satisfaction to the public, will find his situation to be a very lucrative one.   Letters containing proposals may be addressed to the Masters of the Mason Lodges, Inverness."

August 1. The joint committee agreed to let the house and office house to Mr Hay, on the following terms:—The lease to be for twelve years; the rent for the first two years, £50 per annum; for the following three years, £55; and for the remaining seven years, £60—with a break upon twelve months' notice at the end of the first five years—"the option on the part of the Lodges to be made use of only in the event of their being dissatisfied with the conduct of Mr Hay, and being able to satisfy any two respectable gentlemen on the part of Mr Hay that they have good reason for not approving of his conduct." It will be noticed that there is a considerable decrease in the rent paid by Mr Beverley, viz., £65.

Mr Hay was requested to look through the house and make out a note of such repairs and alterations as he shall think absolutely necessary to be made previous to his entering into possession.   Brother

Macdonald was requested to converse with Mrs Be- 179
verley on the subject, and let her know the necessity
for her speedy removal.

Aug. 8. The joint committee approve of a list of
repairs and alterations sent in by Mr Hay, instruct
them to be completed before the first of October, and
request Mr Campbell Mackintosh, their agent, to
make out a lease to Mr Hay on the terms settled at
last meeting.

Nov. 30. " Brother Major Munro presented the
Lodge with a handsome sword, for which the brethren return him their hearty thanks."

The ball and supper alluded to in the minute of
October 23 duly took place.

Dec. 27. A letter from Mrs Beverley was read,
"in which she intimates her intention of removing
to Glasgow with her family, and prayed that the
money collected for her at the Northern Meeting and
in the Lodges at St Andrew's day might not be sunk
on an annuity for her, as was proposed, because it
would be of more service to her and her family if
paid into her hands, as she might help her living in
Glasgow by furnishing a small shop with it, which
being considered by the brethren, they agree to comply with Mrs Beverley's request, and they authorize
the Treasurer to advance to her a small part of the
money previous to her leaving this place, for the
maintenance of her family, and upon his being as-
sured that she is actually quitting this place, and to
pay her the balance that will be then in his hands,
or to order his correspondent in Glasgow to pay it on
her arrival in that city."

The tack with Mr Hay was read and approved,

1792   and delivered to Bailie John Mackintosh to be kept for behoof of the Lodges.

1793   Afterwards the application of Mrs Beverley was considered, and " on the Lodges being satisfied that she shall actually depart for Glasgow," to accede to her request.   In addition to a sum of £45. 3s. already in the hands of the Treasurer for her account, the brethren of the Old Lodge contributed for her £10 12s., making in all, £55. 15s.

May 21. At a committee meeting the balance of the money contributed for the relief of Mrs Beverley and her family was found to be £44. 13s. for the discharge of her house rent and the expense of transporting herself and her family to Glasgow.   The remaining £30 was to be paid to her in Glasgow. The contributions for Mrs Beverley amounted in all to £64. 14s., and were thus made up—

		£	s.	d.
Cash received by Mr Inglis from the Dutchess of Gordon, being the collection made at the Northern Meeting	.	46	17	0
Received from Sir Hector Munro, by the hands of Phineas Mackintosh, Esq.		2	0	0
Baillie Scott	.	1	1	0
Baillie John Mackintosh	.	1	1	0
Major Munro	.	1	1	0
Alex. Fraser, Esq. of Torbreck	.	1	1	0
Lachlan Macgillivray, Esq.	.	1	1	0
Subscriptions of the Old Lodge	.	10	12	0
		£64	14	0

Of this she was paid in different sums from November 1792 to March 1793, £20. 1s. An item on 10th May 1793 is of special interest when contrasted with prices in the present day—" Paid for three barrels coal, 7s." The corresponding price to-day is 6s. 6d.

June 21. " The committee having taken into consideration an offer made to them of £165 sterling for an annuity of £15 sterling yearly on the life of Mrs Grant of Tullochgorum, ... agree to accept the same, and request of Baillie John Mackintosh to correspond with Mr Grant, Lochletter, on the business."

Nov. 30. A committee of both Lodges ordered to meet on 2d December, "to consider measures respecting the conduct of John Hay, their present tenant."

There is no record of the meeting on 2d December, but on 7th December the joint committee recommend their trustees " to accept of John Hay's renunciation as agreed to by the last meeting of both committees," and they recommend the new trustees appointed, as mentioned below, " to let the said inn, and that they meet at least once a fortnight till this business is completed."

At this meeting Bailie John Mackintosh and William Cuming made a representation " that they wished to divest themselves of the property of the new Inn or Mason Lodge in Inverness, and to convey the same to such others of the brethren as may be named, . . . who ought in that case to relieve them of the debts and annuities affecting both Lodges and the said property. The committee are of opinion that this should be done accordingly."

(For new trustees, see page 197.)

Mr Wilson continued tenant of the hotel until his death in 1839. Mr John Grant became the next tenant, entering at Whitsunday 1840, at a rent of £230 annually, and continuing till Martinmas 1848, after which Mr Charles Spinks became tenant, at a rent of £400, subsequently increased to £500 sterling, and continued till Whitsunday 1863, when he retired. The hotel was then let to Mr Jas. Menzies, from Melrose, at the same rent, viz., £500 sterling, and he continued till Whitsunday 1867, when the present worthy occupant, Mr John Menzies, entered into possession.

The affairs of the Lodge were administered by the committee before-named up till the formation of the Friendly Society in 1842, and various money arrangements were carried through, in order to provide the necessary funds for the purchase of additional grounds and extension of the hotel, but there is not much to interest the reader, the minutes being confined to the recital of legal facts and statements of accounts. At the end of the account of St John's Lodge I have given an account of the steps taken, and the gentlemen who interested themselves in the formation of the Friendly Society, and who now hold office, and I shall glance briefly at the nature of the society, and then give a short history of the heritable subjects now held by it. The whole of the Lodge property was, in 1842, made over to the Society, which consisted of twenty-four members, the first-mentioned twelve of whom died, or were struck off the roll, previous to the revision of the rules in 1853.

The names of the original members were—

> John Ferguson, wine merchant.
> John Mactavish, banker.
> John Cook Gordon, solicitor.
> James Smith, bookseller.
> Hugh Innes, merchant.
> James Sutherland, distiller.
> John Grant, innkeeper.
> Alexander Cumming, merchant.
> Donald Mactavish, solicitor.
> James Smith, architect.
> Rev. Alexander Campbell, Petty.
> John Edwards.
> Thomas Ross, merchant.
> Archibald Tait, perfumer.
> John Thomson, banker.
> George Mackay, merchant.
> John Mackay, banker.
> Joseph Mitchell, C.E.
> Robert Naughten, jeweller.
> Alexander Mactavish, Town-Clerk.
> John Grant Manford, writer, Forres.
> Andrew Smith, merchant.
> Kenneth Douglas, bookseller.
> David Prophet, solicitor.

At the first meeting of the society, held on 27th February 1843, Mr John Macandrew, solicitor, was admitted a member, and no further addition was made till 28th March 1853, when Mr James Macpherson, solicitor, was admitted.

The following rules will best give an idea of the nature and aims of the Society. They are excerpts from the revised rules of 1877 :—

"1. This Friendly Society is designated 'THE ST JOHN'S KILWINNING LODGE OF FREEMASONS, INVERNESS, No. 6 OF SCOTLAND'S FRIENDLY SOCIETY," and shall be at all times connected with the said Lodge of Freemasons in the manner after-mentioned. The Registered Office of the Society is the Caledonian Hotel, Church Street, Inverness.

"2. The following parties—1, Joseph Mitchell of Viewhill, Inverness; 2, William Ross Grant, solicitor, there; 3, Charles Spinks, of Seabrook Villa, there; 4, James Anderson, solicitor, there; 5, Henry Cockburn Macandrew, solicitor, there; 6, Andrew Dougall, railway manager, there; 7, Robert Carruthers, junior, publisher, there; 8, Walter Carruthers, wine-merchant, there; 9, James Rose, wine-merchant, there; 10, Alexander Ross, architect, there; 11, Theophilus James Bulkeley, solicitor, Lochmaddy; 12, Charles Innes, solicitor, Inverness; 13, Archibald Thomas Frederick Fraser, clothier, there; and 14, William Jolly, one of her Majesty's Inspectors of Schools, there—are hereby declared to be, with such persons as may be hereafter admitted, the constituent members of the Society, entitled to the benefits and privileges, and bound by and subject to the conditions and obligations hereinafter specified, and which may from time to time be agreed to and enacted by the Society.

" 3. It is declared that the objects of the Society shall be to provide a fund for granting annuities to widows of deceased members during life, and to the orphans of deceased members during minority, until the youngest of the family attain the age of twenty-one years complete ; to maintain and extend the property of the Society ; and to defray the expenses of management of the Society.

" 8. The members of the Society shall, from and after the establishment of these Rules, pay to the Treasurer at the Annual General Meeting of 10th January, the following sums in name of yearly subscription, viz.:—The present members the sum of £4 each, and future members the sum of £6 each : said sums being payable only for a period of ten years from the date of admission of each present or future member respectively ; and after the expiry of said period of ten years, each member the sum of £1.

" 9. Members of the said Lodge of Freemasons not exceeding fifty years of age, in good health, and free from all serious and dangerous bodily ailment, imperfection, or injury, when they apply for admittance, shall be eligible for admission as members of the Society.   Every applicant for admission shall submit to an examination by the medical officer of the Society, and produce a certificate of his health and state of body by his own medical attendant, if he has one ; and the members of the Society shall be the only judges of the effect and import of such certificate, and the report of their own medical officer. In order to maintain the rate of annuity at its present amount at least, the Society shall in the meantime be limited to eighteen members, but without prejudice to this limit being altered from time to time in accordance with the state of the Society's funds.

" 10. The entry money payable by a new member shall be £30 for a person of the age of 21 and under 22, with £2 additional for every year his age exceeds that period.

" 11. The widow of every deceased member shall be entitled to a yearly annuity to be fixed by the Society from time to time, but not exceeding £50 sterling, payable half-yearly during her life ; and orphans of each member surviving his wife, as well as orphans surviving their mothers after their having become widows, shall receive the share which would have been payable to their deceased mother, aye and until the youngest child shall attain the age of twenty-one years, full and complete, but in no case shall any orphan receive any share or annuity after attaining the age of twenty-one years complete.

" 12. In implement of the obligation to make good the deficiency, should it be found that at any time or in any event the ordinary quarter-pence of the said Lodge of Free Masons is insufficient to pay the ordinary and necessary expense thereof, contained in the Title Deeds of the property conveyed by the Lodge to the Society, a yearly sum of not less than £30 shall be paid by the Society to the Treasurer of the Lodge ; and in the event of the Lodge in· any year claiming a larger sum than £30, as due under said obligation, the sum to be paid shall be adjusted between the Lodge and the Society."

The heritable subjects at the time they were made over to the Society were rented at £230 sterling. The transfer was made under burden of a debt amounting to £1400 ; an annuity of £20 to a lady now deceased, and the obligation to make good any deficiency to the Lodge as before mentioned.

In 1845 the Society purchased an adjoining property for £1400, and added it to the hotel, thus increasing the rent to £330.   In 1848 the rent became £400.   In 1858 the Society purchased an adjoining site for £430, and erected buildings upon it to the value of £1700, consisting partly of an addition to the hotel and partly of a shop now let to Messrs Cumming & Campbell, drapers.   This shop was let at Whitsunday 1859 for £60, and the rent of the hotel increased to £500 at Whitsunday following.   In addition to the above sums, the Society has expended in extending and improving the property upwards of £4000—three-fourths of it within the last ten or twelve years.   In 1868 the shop rent was raised to £110, and a lease for ten years granted, and in 1874 the hotel was let for seven years at a rent of £750 per annum.   At Whitsunday 1878 the shop rent increases to £125, at which rent a lease for ten years has been arranged.

Two properties which flank the Society's subjects on either side having come into the market, they have been purchased by the Society.   The larger, on the north side, belonged to Mr Charles Spinks, and was purchased for £3000, though this was considerably under its market value.   Mr Spinks further generously allowed the whole purchase price to remain a burden on it, at 4½ per cent., for five years at least. The gross rental of this purchase is £145.   The property on the south side, between Bank Lane and the Society's property, was purchased for £1630, the gross rental being £92. 2s.   The Society have thus acquired

15

the whole block of property (except a small portion
next Church Street belonging to Miss Naughten),
extending from Church Street to the river side, and
from Bank Lane northwards a distance of about
158 feet.

The property is one likely to rise in value.

The gross rental after Whitsunday next is expected to be £1131

Income from Members—

£1 from nine members . .	£9	
£4 from five members . .	20	
	—	29

Total income . . . £1160

Payments—

Burdens and insurance . .	£105	
Repairs, say	70	
Interest on borrowed money .	315	
Donation to Lodge . .	30	
Management and sundries .	40	
	———	560

Estimated annual surplus of income   £600

The number of members on the Society at
    present is   14
And annuitants   11

With reference to the foregoing statement of the
Lodge Society as it now stands, it may be interesting
to compare the one submitted to the Society by
Provost Ferguson in 1842, he having at that date

held the office of treasurer to the joint Lodges for a period of 25 years :—

Amount at debit at 4 per cent.	.	£1400	0	0
House rent per annum	.	£230 0 0		
Deduct annually for insurance, taxes, and repairs . .		30 0 0		

Free Rental	.	£200 0 0		
Contribution of £1 per quarter for 30 members annually		120 0 0		

Annual Income .		£320 0 0		
Deduct interest of £1400 at 4 per cent. . . .		56 0 0		

Free Income	£264 0 0		

Interest of this sum for four years at 4 per cent.	£42	4	10	
Interest of this sum for three years .	31	13	7	
Interest of this sum for two years .	21	2	5	
Interest of this sum for one year .	10	11	2	

Amount of interest .	.	£105	12	0
Add principal, four years at £264 per annum		1056	0	0

Principal and interest .	.	£1161	12	0
New entrants, supposed to average two per annum, for four years, at £30 each		240	0	0

Funds at Martinmas 1846 .	£1401	12	0	
Debt at same date .	.	1400	0	0

Calculating interest at 5 per cent. the funds would be increased £27.

It thus appears that in four years, or at Martinmas 1846, the debt due by the Society will be paid
up and the free income annually will then be—

Rent of house, as before . . .	£230	0	0
Deduct for contingencies . . .	30	0	0
Free Rental . . .	£200	0	0
Contributions annually by 38 members at £4 each	152	0	0
Annual Income . .	£352	0	0

At the beginning of this volume will be found a
list of the present members of St John's. The number is fully as great as in former years, and the spirit
is well sustained. A sum of £30 a year is allowed
from the Friendly Society, which helps to pay the
ordinary working expenses and the annual dinner on
St John's day and St Andrew's day. The revenue
from fees and quarter-pence is considerable. The
Lodge lately procured a new set of fittings, new
furniture, and other appliances, which were used for
the first time on St John's day 1877.

A few days ago, in examining the Tyler's box,
wherein are kept the various insignia and tools, the
old jewels of St Andrew's Lodge were discovered:
being the set purchased for £1. 8s. 5d., to replace
those alleged to have been stolen by the Duke of
Cumberland's serjeants at the time of Culloden.
They consist of six jewels, viz.:—Master's square and
compass, bearing inscription "St Andrew's Kilwinning Lodge, Inverness, 30th Nov. 1749;" Depute-
Master's square; Past Master's jewel; Senior and
Junior Warden's jewels; Secretary's jewel. They are
of the simplest form, having been cut out of plates
of thin metal, the Master's and one or two of the
more important being neatly chased. It may be
mentioned that the present Tyler, John Fotheringham, has worthily held office for 25 years; and that
the same office was also held by his father for 26 years,
the two having thus held office for upwards of half-a-
century.

REGISTER OF THE MASTERS, WARDENS, SECRETARIES, AND TREASURERS OF THE ST JOHN'S OLD INVERNESS KILWINNING LODGE, NO. 6.

	MASTERS.	SENIOR WARDENS	JUNIOR WARDENS	SECRETARIES.	TREASURERS.
1678	Wm. MacIntosh (brother of the Laird of MacIntosh)	Alexander Nicolson	Andrew Ross ...	...	Donald Ross
1681	do.	do.	do. ...		William Hendrie
1684	do.	do.	John M'Bean ...		Andrew Ross
1692	James Barbour of Auldowry	John Reid	John Heburn ...		do.
1699	John Heburn ...	do. ...	Robert Nicolson		do.
1701	James Dick ...	Andrew Ross ...	William Cumming		Alexander Tulloch
1702	do.	Robert Nicolson	Alexander Tulloch		John Thomson
1716	Andrew Scott ...	James Dick ...	John Dick ...		do.
1718	do.	Robert Ross ...	Thomas Tulloch		Thomas Tulloch
1719	William M'Lise (or M'Gillies)	Donald Tulloch	do. ...		do.
1722	John Nicolson ...	Donald M'Lise...	John M'Bean ...		Alexander Fraser
1724	John M'Bean, sheriff-clerk	do. ...	John Jackson ...		John Jackson
1733	Bailie William MacIntosh	John Dunbar ...	Alexander Fraser		Alexander Fraser
1735	John M'Bean, sheriff-clerk	do. ...	do. ...		do.

	MASTERS.	SENIOR WARDENS	JUNIOR WARDENS	SECRETARIES.	TREASURERS.
1736	Geo. Cuthbert of Castle-hill	John Dunbar ...	Donald M'Lise...	...	Alexander Fraser
1737	do.	do. ...	John Tulloch ...	Charles Falconar	do.
1738	do.	Robert Nicolson	Donald M'Lise...	Alexander M'Intosh	Charles M'Culloch, gunsmith
1739	Arch. Grahame, officer of excise	do. ...	William Grant...	do. ...	do.
1740	Dun. Fraser, merchant	Cha. Falconar, wrytar	Andrew Brereton	John Dunbar ...	do.
1741	Geo. Cuthbert of Castle-hill	Donald M'Liss ...	Alex. Fraser (Alex. Simson alias Fraser)	Alexander M'Intosh, messenger	John Monro, couper
1742	do.	Archibald Grahame	Don. Fraser, squair-wright in Inverness	John M'Lean ...	do.
1743	Archibald Grahame	Donald M'Liss...	John Monro, couper	do.	do.
1744	do.	do. ...	Robert Nicolson	do.	Alexander Fraser
1745	Duncan Fraser, merchant and Provost	do. ...	Donald Fraser ..	do.	do.
1746	Archibald Grahame	Humph. Colquhoun	John Monro	John Dunbar ...	do.
1747	do.	John Bailie, Writer to the Signet	Robert Nicolson	John M'Lean, writer in Inverness	John Fraser (son to Alex. Fraser, mason)
1748	do.	John Tulloch ...	Robt. Cuthbert, shoemaker	Thomas Tulloch	do.
1749	do.	do. ...	John Fraser ...	John Dunbar ...	Thomas Tulloch
1750	do.	Donald M'Liss...	do.	do. ...	do.
1751	John MackLean, writer in Inverness	John Dunbar ...	Wm. Cranston (formerly apprentice to Don. M'Lise)	Gillies Ker, schoolmaster at Moy, in Strathnairn	Donald M'Pherson
1752	Donald M'Liss ...	do. ...	John Fraser ...	do.	do.
1753	Duncan Forbes, merchant in Inverness	John Fraser ...	Thomas Tulloch	John Dunbar ...	do.
1754		Gillies Kerr ...	Robt. Edwards, merchant	Duncan Grant, writer	do.

	MASTERS.	SENIOR WARDENS	JUNIOR WARDENS	SECRETARIES.	TREASURERS.
1755	James Geddes, merchant in Inverness	Wm. Cuming, glazier in Inverness	John Fraser ...	Donald M'Bean, vintner	Don. M'Pherson
1756	Duncan Forbes ...	Robt. Edwards, merchant in Inverness	do.	Duncan Grant ...	do.
1757	Wm. Cuming, glazier	Gillies Kerr ...	do. ...	Donald M'Bean	do.
1758	do. ...	John Fraser ...	Duncan Grant ...	do. ...	do.
1759	Duncan Forbes ...	Duncan Grant, writer	Robt. Anderson, silversmith	Hugh Munro, merchant, Inverness	do.
1760	Duncan Grant, writer	John Gilzean, malster	Joseph Purdy, overseer of the salmon fishings	John M'Pherson, merchant	do.
1761	do. ...	Robert Anderson	William Henderson, bleacher in Inverness	Donald M'Bean, son to Donald M'Bean, vintner	do.
1762	Duncan Forbes ...	John Baillie, W.S.	Simon Fraser, baxter	John Fraser ...	do.
1763	Robt. Anderson, silver-smith	Robt. Man, merchant in Inverness	William Henderson	Duncan Grant ...	...
1764	Captain John Gregor	Joha Fraser ...	Simon Fraser ...	Duncan Forbes...	...
1765	do. ...	Alexander Munro	Wm. Welsh, tanner	do. ...	Duncan Forbes
1768	do. ...	do. ...	Jno Gilzean, malster	do. ...	William Cuming
1769	do. ...	do. ...	Donald Mackintosh, shipmaster	Thos. Young, tanner	William Welsh
1771	do. ...	do. ...	John Gilzean ...	do. ...	David Blair, sadler
1772	do. ...	do. ...	William Welsh	do. ...	John Collie, excise officer
1773	Duncan Fraser ...	do. ...	do. ...	do. ...	do.
1774	Captain John Gregor	do. ...	Sam. Ancrum, cooper	do. ...	Wm. Fraser, vintner
1775	Robert Anderson...	do. ...	Thomas Young,...	John Collie, officer of excise	Simon Fraser
1776	do. ...		do. ...	do. ...	W. Sharp, bookseller

	MASTERS.	SENIOR WARDENS	JUNIOR WARDENS	SECRETARIES.	TREASURERS.
1777	Robert Anderson	Alexander Munro	Thomas Young	John Collie, officer of excise	Wm. Fraser, writer
1778	Captain John Gregor	do. ...	do. ...	do. ...	Kenneth Mackenzie
1779	Robert Anderson...	Thomas Young...	William Welsh...	do. ...	do.
1780	do.	do. ...	Simon Fraser ...	William Welsh	do.
1782	Thomas Young ...	Simon Fraser, merchant	Wm. Fraser, glover	Kenneth M'Kenzie	John Ettles, vintner
1783	do.	do. ...	D nald Mackintosh	Thomas Munro...	Arthur Sinclair
1784	do.	do. ...	Alex. M'Leod, sadler	do. ...	James Blair, from Dundee
1785	Capt. John M'Gregor. 3d American Regt.	do. ...	do. ...	do.	do.
1787	do.	Alex. M'Leod, sadler	Andrew Lauchlan	do. ...	John Mackenzie
1789	Wm. Cuming, glazier	Andrew Lauchlan	John M'Kenzie...	James Reid, jun., merchant	James Macdonald
1791	Thomas Young ...	do. ...	do. ...	do. ...	Henry Andrews
1792	Alex. M'Leod, sadler	John M'Kenzie	FarquharMacdonald, surveyor of customs	James Macdonald, merchant	
1793	Simon Fraser of Farraline	William Welsh	do. ...	Henry Andrews	William Grant
1794	Andrew Lauchlan	Farquhar M'Donald	Henry Andrews	James Suter (from Forres)	Charles Jameson, silversmith
1795	Thomas Young ...	Henry Andrews, merchant	William Grant...	Alex. Macdonell	Donald Macpherson
1796	Andrew Lauchlan	do. ...	Bailie Don. M'Pherson	do. ...	Hugh Cobban, merchant
1797	William Welsh, tanner	William Grant...	do. ...	do. ...	do.
1798	Farquhar MacDonald	Donald MacPherson, merchant	Charles Jamieson	do. ...	Alex. MacGillivray
1799	Donald Macpherson	William Grant...	Alex. MacDonell	Donald Macpherson, writer	John Simpson, merchant

	MASTERS.	SENIOR WARDENS	JUNIOR WARDENS	SECRETARIES.	TREASURERS.
1800	John Mackenzie ...	Alex. MacDonell	Hugh Cobban ...	Donald Macpherson, writer	John Simpson, merchant
1801	William Grant ...	Hugh Cobban ...	John Simpson ...	do. ...	George Urquhart
1804	do. ...	do. ...	Alex. MacGillivray	do. ...	do.
1805	Alexander Macdonell	John Simpson ...	do. ...	William Chisholm	Alexander Murray
1806	Hugh Cobban ..	Alex. MacGillivray	James Suter ...	do. ...	do.
1807	William Grant ..	do. ...	George Urquhart	Alexander Murray	Alex. Fraser, baker
1808	Dond. MacPherson	James Suter ...	Alexander Smith	do. ...	do.
1809	do. ...	Alexander Smith	John Smith ...	Colin Kemp ...	do.
1810	Alexander Smith..	John Smith ...	Alexander Dallas	do. ...	Robert Nicolson
1811	do. ...	Alexander Fraser	do. ...	do. ...	do.
1812	do. ...	James Lyon ...	Arthur Cooper ...	John Edwards ...	do.
1813	James Lyon, merchant	Arthur Cooper ...	John Edwards...	Lewis Grant ...	John Stewart
1815	John Edwards ...	Lewis Grant ...	Alex. Shepperd, solr.	John Mackay ...	do.
1816	do. ...	do. ...	do. ...	John Munro ...	do.
1817	Alex. Smith, of Dellmore	James Errol Gray	Alexander Cumming	James Suter, jun.	John Ferguson, wine-merchant
1818	Alexander Shepperd	do. ...	Robert Murray...	John Munro ...	do.
1819	Farquhar MacDonald	Alexander Cumming	do. ...	do. ...	do.
1821	John Edwardes ..	do. ...	Robert Smith ...	Don. F. Mackenzie, solicitor	do.
1822	Alex. Cumming, mercer	Robt. Smith of Dellmore	Thomas Ross ...	do.	do.
1823	Robt. Smith, solicitor	Thos. Ross, merchant	John MacIntosh	do.	do.
1824	do. ...	J. Thomson, banker	do. ...	do.	do.
1825	do ...	do. ...	J. Cook Gordon	do.	do.
1827	do. ...	George Simpson	Robt.Smith, solicitor	do.	do.
1829	Rob.Smith of Delimore	Robt. Smith, solicitor	J. G. Manford ...	do.	do.
1830	do. ...	J. G. Manford ...	R.Naughten.jeweller	do.	do.
1831	do. ...	do. ...	Jas. Dickson, seedsman	do.	do.

	MASTERS.	SENIOR WARDENS	JUNIOR WARDENS	SECRETARIES.	TREASURERS.
1832	Rob. Smith of Dellmore	James Dickson	John Fraser	Donald F. Mackenzie	John Ferguson
1834	James Dickson	Wm. Munro, M.D.	William M'Cargow	Jno. Mactavish, solr.	do.
1835	do.	do.	Wm. Lyon, merchant	Ranald Stalker, do.	do.
1836	do.	Wm. Lyon, merchant	Archibald Tait	do.	do.
1837	Alex. Mactavish, solr.	do.	J. Fraser, Inchberry	Ken. Douglas	do.
1839	do.	do.	John Fraser, Sheuglie	do.	do.
1840	do.	do.	And. Smith, clothier	do.	do.
1841	John Thomson, banker	And. Smith, clothier	Arch. Tait, merchant	J. Cook Gordon, solr.	do.
1843	do.	Thos. Ross, merchant	Jno. Mactavish, solr.	do.	do.
1844	do.	do.	do.	David Prophet, solr.	do.
1846	Thos. Ross, wd.-mercht.	R. Naughten, jeweller	do.	do.	Arch. Tait, merchant
1848	do.	do.	Joseph Mitchell, C.E.	do.	do.
1851	do.	do.	Kenneth Douglas	do.	do.
1852	do.	do.	Jas. Macpherson, solr.	do.	do.
1855	do.	do.	do.	Wm. R. Grant, solr.	do.
1856	do.	James Macpherson	W. Simpson, mercht.	do.	do.
1861	James Macpherson	William Simpson	T. Watts, collector of customs	do.	do.
1863	do.	Thomas Watts	Alex Dallas, solicitor	do.	do.
1864	do.	William Lawrie	Daniel J. Blyth	do.	do.
1866	do.	do.	Charles Innes	do.	do.
1868	Charles Innes	Theo. J. Bulkeley	Lewis A. Inkson	do.	do.
1870	do.	Lewis A. Inkson	Alexander Ross	Theo. J. Bulkeley	do.
1871	do.	John Macewen	James Rose, wine-merchant	William Tavish Mac-tavish, solicitor	do.
1872	Alexander Ross	James Rose	John Colvin	Don. Reid, solicitor	Hugh Rose, solicitor
1873	do.	John Macewen	Walter Carruthers	do.	do.
1874	do.	Jas. Rose	do.	do.	do.
1875	do.	Walter Carruthers	George G. Allan	do.	do.
1876	do.	Geo. G. Allan	William Burns	do.	do.
1877	Walter Carruthers	do.	do.	do.	do.

REGISTER OF THE MASTERS, WARDENS, SECRETARIES, AND TREASURERS OF ST ANDREW'S KILWINNING LODGE, NO. 31.

	MASTERS.	SENIOR WARDENS	JUNIOR WARDENS	SECRETARIES.	TREASURERS.
1735	Lachlan Mackintosh, merchant, Inverness	...	...	John Taylor	...
1737	Wm. Duff, postmaster	Henry Rose of Merkness	Angus Mackintosh	...	...
...	Lachlan Mackintosh, merchant, Inverness	...	...	...	...
1739	William Duff of Kellymure (Secretary or Postmaster?)	...	...	...	...
...	Evan Baillie of Abriachan	John Shaw, merchant in Inverness	Andrew Monro		...
...	do.	Angus Mackintosh, merchant	John Shaw, merchant		...
1745	Daniel Barbour of Aldowrie	...	...		...
...	William Duff of Muirton, late master	...	...		...
...	Collector Alex. Colvill, do.	...	...		...
...	Evan Baillie of Abriachan, do.	...	...		...

	MASTERS.	SENIOR WARDENS	JUNIOR WARDENS	SECRETARIES.	TREASURERS.
1748	Collector Alex. Colvill	Evan Baillie ...	William Chisholm ...	Wm. Baillie ...	John Taylor
1749	do. ... Andrew Monro ...	do. ...	do. ...	do. ...	do.
1750	Wm. Duff of Muirton	Dr Chisolm (afterwards Provost)	John Grant ...	do. ...	William Baillie
...	(Capt. Alex. Mackenzie of General Marjoribank's Regiment, a former Master of this Lodge)	...	...	...	...
1751	William Chisholm	John Grant ...	Alexander Duff	...	do.
1752	John Grant ...	Alexander Duff	John Baillie ...	Alexander Fraser	John Baillie
1753	Hon. Alex. Colvil	Evan Baillie ...	William Chisholm ...	do. ...	Alex. Fraser
1754	Evan Baillie ...	John Grant ...	Alexander Duff	do. ...	do.
1755	Alexander Duff ...	William Chisholm ...	William Baillie	James Gordon ...	do.
1756	William Chisholm ...	Wm. Duff of Muirton	John Grant ...	do. ...	James Gordon
1757	Duncan Fraser of Achnagairn	do. ...	do. ...	do. ...	do.
1758	Wm. Duff of Muirton	John Grant ...	Alexander Duff	do. ...	do.
1759	John Grant ...	Evan Baillie of Abriachan	Dr Chisholm ...	do. ...	do.
1760	Evan Baillie of Abriachan	Wm. Duff of Muirton	do. ...	do. ...	do.
1761	Dr William Chisholm	do. ... of Achnagairn	John Grant ...	do. ...	do.
1762	Hon. Alex. Colvil	Duncan Fraser of Achnagairn	do. ...	do. ...	do.
1763	Dr William Chisholm	John Grant	Col. Forbes M'Bean	Alexander Grant	Alexander Grant
1764	Wm. Duff of Muirton	Col. Forbes M'Bean	Hugh Falconar, merchant in Inverness	do. ...	do.
1765	Dr William Chisolme	Hugh Falconar	Capt. Alexander Duff	do.	do.

	MASTERS.	SENIOR WARDENS	JUNIOR WARDENS	SECRETARIES.	TREASURERS.
1766	Dr William Chisolme	Hugh Falconar	Capt. Alex. Fraser	Alexander Grant	Alexander Grant
1767	William Duff, late old Master	Captain Alex. Duff	Alex. Grant, sheriff-clerk	do. ...	do.
1768	Capt. Alexander Duff	Hugh Falconar	do. ...	do. ...	do.
1769	Capt Wm. M'Gillivray Alexander Baillie of Dochfour	Alexander Baillie Roderick Mackenzie	Roderick Mackenzie Hugh Falconar	William Inglis	John Mackintosh do.
1770	Dr William Chisolme	William Mackintosh Bailie William Mackintosh	Alex. Mackintosh	William Cuthbert	do.
1771	Major Alexander Duff		do. ...	do. ...	do.
1772	James Baillie ...	Alex. Mackintosh	Capt. Bannatyne	do. ...	do.
1773	Major James Chisolm	do. ...	do. ...	do. ...	do.
1774	Capt. Alex. Duff ...	Captain Bannatyne	William Inglis ...	do. ...	do.
1775	Capt. Wm. Bannatyne, tacksman of Balloan	William Inglis ...	Bailie John Mackintosh	William Scott ...	do.
1776	Alex. Baillie of Dochfour	do. ...	do. ...	do. ...	do.
1777	Alex. Fraser of Culduthel (died in office)	do. ...	do. ...	do. ...	John Shaw
1778	Alexander Baillie	do. ...	do. ...	do.	do.
1779	William Chisholm	do. ...	do. ...	do.	do.
1780	Bailie William Inglis	Bailie John Mackintosh	William Cuthbert	do.	do.
1781	Bailie Jno. Mackintosh	Wm. Cuthbert—died	William Scott	do.	do.
1782		Capt. Thos. Walcoat	do. ...	do. ...	...
1783	Capt. Thomas Walcoat Bailie Alexander Mackintosh	William Scott ...	Dr James Macleod do. ...	do. 3o. ...	do. do.
1784	Major George Munro	do. ...	John Baillie of Duneen	Charles Jamieson	do.
1785	Simon Fraser of Farraline	do. ...		do. ...	Robert Rose

	MASTERS.	SENIOR WARDENS	JUNIOR WARDENS	SECRETARIES.	TREASURERS.
1786	Provost Wm. Chisolm	William Scott ...	John Baillie of Dunean	Charles Jamieson	Robert Rose
1787	Major James Chisholm	do. ...	James Fraser of Culduthel	do. ...	do.
1788	Bailie William Inglis	James Fraser of Culduthel	Angus Mackintosh of Holm	do. ...	do.
1789	Bailie Jno. Mackintosh	do. ...	do. ...	do.	do.
1790	Capt. Walcott ...	do. ...	do. ...	do.	do.
1791	James Fraser of Culduthel	John Baillie of Dunain	do. ...	do.	do.
1792	Capt. John Baillie of Dunain	Angus Mackintosh of Holm	Wm. Mackintosh of Aberarder	do. ...	William Wilson
1793	Angus Mackintosh of Holm	Wm. Mackintosh of Aberarder	Arthur Forbes of Culloden	do. ...	do.
1794	William Inglis ...	Arthur Forbes of Culloden	William Jamieson	Thomas Gilzean	do.
1795	Arthur Forbes of Culloden	Charles Jamieson	Captain Alpin Grant	do. ...	do.
1796	Capt. Thomas Walcott	do. ...	do. ...	do.	do.
1797	Wm. Scott of Seabank	do. ...	do. ...	do.	do.
1798	Provost John Mackintosh	do. ...	do. ...	do.	do.
1799	Angus Mackintosh of Holm	do. ...	do. ...	do. ...	do.
1800	William Inglis ...	do. ...	Dr James Robertson	do. ...	do.
1801	Arthur Forbes of Culloden	Captain Alpin Grant	...	do. ...	do.
1802	do. (deceased)	do. ...	do. ...	do.	do.
1803	Hon. Col. Archibald Fraser of Lovat	do. ...	do. ...	do.	do.

	MASTERS.	SENIOR WARDENS	JUNIOR WARDENS	SECRETARIES.	TREASURERS.
1804	Provost John Mackintosh	Dr James Robertson	Colin Munro ...	Alex. Mackenzie ...	William Wilson
1805	Dr James Robertson	Colin Munro ...	Captain Donald Mackenzie of Newhall	do. ...	do.
1806	Hon. Archd. Fraser of Lovat	do.	do. ...	do. ...	do.
1807	Angus Mackintosh of Holm	do.	do. ...	do. ...	do.
1808	Thos. Gilzean of Bunachton, Provost of Inverness	do.	do. ...	do. ...	do.
1809	Simon Fraser of Farraline, Sheriff of the County of Inverness (died in office)	do.		do. ...	do.
1810	Angus Mackintosh of Holm	do. ...	do. ...	do.	Alex. Mackintosh
1811	Dr James Robertson of Inverness	Dr Kennedy ...	William Fraser of Culbokie	do.	do.
1812	do. ...	do.	do. ...	do.	do.
1813	Angus Mackintosh of Holm	do.	do. ...	do.	do.
1814	Provost Thos. Gilzean	do.	do. ...	do.	do.
1815	Dr James Robertson	do.	Provost Jas. Grant of Bught	do.	do.
1816	Provost Thos. Gilzean of Bunachton	do.	do. ...	do.	do.
1817	do. ...	do.	do. ...	do.	do.
1818	do. ...	do.	do. ...	do.	do.
1819	do. ...	do.	do. ...	do.	do.
1820	do. ...	do.	do. ...	do.	do.

	MASTERS.	SENIOR WARDENS	JUNIOR WARDENS	SECRETARIES.	TREASURERS.
1821	Provost Thos. Gilzean of Bunachton	Dr Kennedy ...	Provost Jas. Grant of Bught	Alex. Mackenzie	Alex. Mackintosh
1822	do.	do.	do.	do. (of Woodside)	do.
1823	do.	Provost Jas. Grant of Bught	Affleck Fraser of Culduthel		do.
1824	do.	do.	do.	do.	do.
1825	do.	do.	do.	do.	do.
...	Provost Gilzean acted as Master until the Lodges were united in 1839.				

REGISTER OF THE ST MARY'S CALEDONIAN OPERATIVE LODGE OF FREEMASONS, No. 339 OF SCOTLAND.

This Lodge, as mentioned at page 4, was established in 1843. The names of the petitioners for the Charter being—John Batchen, of St John's, Forres; Alexander Fraser, of Clachnacuddin, Inverness; John Russel, of St John's, Forres; John Fraser, St Ninian's, Nairn; David Spence, St Nicholas, Aberdeen; Alexander Thomson, St John's, Montrose; William Watson, St John's, Forres. Date of Charter, 8th May 1843. This Lodge has been very successful, and has a large number of members. Since its formation it has initiated 629 members.

	MASTERS.	SENIOR WARDENS.	JUNIOR WARDENS.	SECRETARIES.	TREASURERS.
1843	John Batchen	John Russel	John Fraser	Alexander Thomson	David Spence
1844	do.	do.	do.	do.	do.
1845	do.	do.	do.	do.	do.
1846	do.	do.	do.	do.	do.
1847	do.	James Macpherson	John Ross	Alexander Fraser	John Machendry
1849	John Fraser	do.	do.	do.	do.
1850	do.	John Ross	John Fraser	do.	James Park
1851	John Batchen	John Fraser	Alexander Thomson	do.	Arch. Johnston
1852	do.	James Urquhart	Alexander Gordon	do.	Alexander Macinnes
1853	do.	do.	William Mackenzie	do.	do.
1854	do.	Alexander Gordon	do.	do.	John Russel
1855	John Ross	William Mackenzie	Francis Wilson	do.	do.

	MASTERS.	SENIOR WARDENS.	JUNIOR WARDENS.	SECRETARIES.	TREASURERS.
1856	John Ross	Francis Wilson	Andrew Fraser	Alex. Fraser	John Russel
1857	Andrew Fraser	John Russel	Donald Macdonald	do.	John Munro
1858	do.	Donald Macdonald	John Ellis	do.	Francis Wilson
1859	do.	John Ellis	D. J. Blyth	John Batchen	do.
1860	Arch. Johnston	do.	do.	John Sutherland	do.
1861	do.	do.	Alexander Ellis	Hugh Munro	William Johnston
1862	do.	do.	do.	do.	do.
1863	do.	do.	John Cook	do.	do.
1864	do.	John Cook	do.	do.	Andrew Fraser
1865	William Mackenzie	do.	James Hutcheson	do.	do.
1866	do.	do.	William Martin	do.	William Mackenzie
1867	do.	do.	John S. Mackay	Samuel Higgie	Charles Macfarlane
1868	do.	John Cameron	Peter Falconer	Duff Kennedy	do.
1869	John Ellis	Andrew Gunn	Donald Fraser	do.	Donald Mackintosh
1870	do.	Donald Fraser	Fraser Rennie	do.	do.
1871	do.	John Cook	William Martin	do.	do.
1872	do.	do.	D. M. Hay	John Pocock	do.
1873	do.	do.	John Cameron	John Balfour	George Millar
1874	do.	do.	do.	do.	Alex. Macpherson
1875	do.	do.	W. M. Snowie	do.	John Tulloch
1876	John B. Falconer	George Smith	William Simpson	do.	Harrold Paterson
1877	do.	William Simpson	William Robertson	do.	do.
1878	George Smith	do.	William Dunbar	Duncan Rose	do.

www.ingramcontent.com/pod-product-compliance
Lightning Source LLC
Chambersburg PA
CBHW031426270326
41930CB00007B/592